Voice and Tone Strategy
Connecting with People through Content

John Caldwell

Voice and Tone Strategy
Connecting with People through Content
Copyright © 2020 John Caldwell

All rights reserved. No part of this book may be reproduced or transmitted in any form or by any means without the prior written permission of the copyright holder, except for the inclusion of brief quotations in a review.

Disclaimer

The information in this book is provided on an "as is" basis, without warranty. While every effort has been taken by the author and XML Press in the preparation of this book, the author and XML Press shall have neither liability nor responsibility to any person or entity with respect to any loss or damages arising from the information contained herein.

This book contains links to third-party web sites that are not under the control of the author or XML Press. The author and XML Press are not responsible for the content of any linked site. Inclusion of a link in this book does not imply that the author or XML Press endorses or accepts any responsibility for the content of that third-party site.

Credits

Series Producer and Editor:	Scott Abel
Series Cover Design:	Marc Posch
Publisher:	Richard Hamilton

Trademarks

XML Press and the XML Press logo are trademarks of XML Press.

All terms mentioned in this book that are known to be trademarks or service marks have been capitalized as appropriate. Use of a term in this book should not be regarded as affecting the validity of any trademark or service mark.

XML Press
Laguna Hills, California
http://xmlpress.net

First Edition
ISBN: 978-1-937434-68-7 (print)
ISBN: 978-1-937434-69-4 (ebook)

Table of Contents

Preface v
1. What is Voice and Tone? 1
   Understanding character, voice, and tone 1
   Where voice and tone live in a content strategy 4
   Marketing and product voice 5
   The importance of relationships 6
2. A Simple Framework for Voice and Tone 9
   Start by setting a goal for your voice and tone 11
   Building block #1: Customer needs and desires 13
   Building block #2: Voice attributes 16
   Building block #3: Principles for voice 17
   Building block #4: Examples 19
3. Building Block 1: Needs and Desires (but mostly desires) 21
   Vision and goal 21
   Desires are the most important strategic target 22
   Using storytelling to discover customer desires 25
   Building a list of customer needs and desires 27
   Validate what you think you know 29
   Narrow to the best opportunities for voice 31
   Declare your own desires in the relationship 32
   Understand human nature, not just characteristics 33
   A strategic foundation for voice and tone 34
4. Building Block 2: Defining an Archetype and Attributes 37
   Focus on the voice of your character 37
   Use a modern archetype to identify your character 38
   Create a set of voice attributes 40
   Put guardrails around your attributes 42
   Consider tone 44
   Test your attributes before moving forward 45
5. Building Block 3: Crafting Principles to Guide Your Voice 47
   Know the difference between a principle and an attribute 47
   Craft principles with writers in mind 49
   Make sure your principles are strategic 50
   Go for the aspirational 51

    Treat your principles like an open toolbox 54
    Create a subset of principles for specific projects and priorities 55
6. Flex Voice and Tone 59
    How do voice and tone flex? 59
    Build a voice flex framework 60
    Flexing tone 65
    Deciding whether to flex voice or tone 68
    Flex frameworks and expanding products or services 69
7. Building Block 4: The Power of Examples 71
    Start with "just-dos" 72
    Create examples to inspire and instruct 73
    Workshop your examples 74
    Present your examples for highest impact 75
    Use outside examples 78
    Test your examples 78
8. Style and Structure 79
    Voice and tone drive style and structure 79
    If you don't already have a style guide, make one 81
    Create a word list 82
    Create a quick reference guide 83
    Set rules for structured content to establish your voice 84
    Allow style and structure to evolve 86
9. The Roll Out 89
    Create a presentation that tells the story of your strategy 89
    Take your presentation on a road show 93
    Start working with content creators to get things rolling 94
    Use what you learn and start version two 95
    Strategy is king. Spread the word 96
10. Epilogue 99
    Master the power of story 99
    The future of voice and tone could be AI 99
    Finally, have a look at my strategy for this book 101
    Acknowledgements 105
References 107
Glossary 111
Index 113

Preface

Connections. We all want them. We seek them in our everyday lives, in our relationships with people, places and things. Emotion is at the heart of any meaningful connection, and how we talk to each other taps into it. Our character, brought to life through our voice, is the most powerful tool we have to connect with people, especially when it comes to connecting on an emotional level.

Indeed, if two products offer essentially the same benefits, the one that taps into emotional needs stands a better chance of success. Winning products succeed by creating lasting relationships with customers, who speak positively about the experience you provide to friends, family members, and even strangers. That's why a formal voice and tone strategy is important to the success of a website, product, platform, or service.

Content strategy comes in many forms and plays different roles on the stage or website and product design. A common definition for a broader strategy is the auditing, planning, structuring, and delivering of content across a customer experience end-to-end. But that's not what this book is about. This book focuses on the role of a voice and tone strategy as a part of a successful content strategy. *Voice and Tone Strategy: Connecting with Customers through Content* examines the role of voice and tone in creating exceptional customer relationships and explores how to create a strategy that addresses customer needs.

In the past, a transactional relationship with customers was sufficient. A simple experience that delivered a clear benefit, such as extra money in their pocket or the easy completion of a task, was all you needed to satisfy and retain existing customers.

But times have changed. Today, more than ever, consumers gravitate toward—and increasingly, crave—meaningful experiences. Consumers develop a strong connection to brands they perceive as thoughtful. They are often overwhelmed with too much irrelevant information, and in those situations, they may prefer to minimize interaction with your brand. Voice and tone can help you strengthen the affinity consumers feel toward your brand, allowing you to build a relationship that will decrease the likelihood that they'll defect to your competitors.

Video game companies, real estate agencies, financial platforms, and restaurants differentiate themselves from the competition by leveraging emotional connections and encouraging engagement. Customers may not think of it this way, but the reality is, they often respond positively to meaningful relationships with the products and services they choose. That's because they want the connection. Voice and tone can deliver the trust and experiences that make those connections real and create loyal customers.[1]

Hungry for tacos? Those too can come with a side of human connection. When you go to the King Taco located at 3rd and Ford Blvd. in East Los Angeles on a Saturday night, you're presented with a choice: Get served at the counter inside the restaurant, or wait for up to an hour at the taco truck parked out front. That's right, they have their own taco truck permanently situated next to the building. They don't drive it anywhere.

Why would hungry taco fans wait for an hour to get the same tacos they can get right away just steps inside the door? Pulitzer Prize-winning food critic Jonathan Gold has an answer. "You're almost eating [the taco] in one continuous motion from the guy to the grill to the counter," he says in the documentary *City of Gold*. "I know it's overly romantic."

Perhaps. But his point is that the taco lovers don't just want the tacos. They want an experience, one in which they sense that they're part of a relationship. At the truck, they hear the meat grilling, watch the sauce being sloshed over it, and make smalltalk with the cook as he delivers their meal through the window. King Taco's self-disruptive taco truck is an adroit maneuver; a tactic that gives hungry taco lovers what they really want.

Think about all the experiences you've had dining out. Which experiences do you remember the most? Which restaurants do you talk about with friends and return to again and again. When mentioned by someone else, which restaurants cause you to exclaim with enthusiasm, "I love that place!"

---

[1] See "Don't Mistake Habit For Loyalty: 5 Trends Driving Loyalty Programs That Create Customers For Life" by Mary Meehan for an exploration of customer loyalty.

There's a good chance it's the eateries where the food is great, and the experience was memorable. Maybe the owner or the chef made an effort to get to know you a bit. They connected with you personally, and treated you like a friend. You might recall it as good service. But, was it more than that? The food was the magic, but how it was presented and served brought additional meaning to the experience.

There's a lot more to a successful voice and tone strategy than just being human and friendly. To connect with people you need to understand what they need and want, especially as those needs vary across touchpoints with different goals. This is where a framework for flexing your voice—adjusting how you talk so its appropriate for the experience—plays an important role.

To build a bond with consumers, you need to position your brand as human. For it to seem real, your character, brought to life through its voice, must also have something at stake. Bringing your own humanity to the relationship is as important as recognizing the needs of your customers.

As a leader of voice and tone strategy development on Intuit's popular TurboTax, QuickBooks, and Mint brands for well over a decade, I can say with confidence that no problem space is more charged with emotion than the world of money and personal finances. Nowhere else did I learn more about the value of creating relationships with customers based on our shared humanity—the universal truth that we are all in this together and must come together to conquer life's many challenges.

The strategic use of voice and tone gives you the opportunity to craft groundbreaking customer experiences. If you're a content designer, UX writer, or content strategist working on customer facing content, you will benefit from the approach covered in this book. I explain the basics of voice and tone and show you how to use storytelling techniques to connect with others. I describe how to build a strategic framework with four building blocks: customer needs, voice and tone attributes, principles, and aspirational examples. And I describe a framework for flexing voice and tone.

CHAPTER 1
What is Voice and Tone?

Your voice is your personality, and your tone is your mood.

—Kristina Adams[2]

In this book, I show you how to be strategic with voice and tone. I present a framework, apply storytelling techniques, and walk you through the steps to build a solid voice and tone strategy and roll it out in your organization. But before I do that, I need to define character, voice and tone. I'll be talking about *voice* and *tone*, not just *tone of voice*. Voice and tone are different, though they're not mutually exclusive.

Understanding character, voice, and tone

You may be employed as a copywriter, user experience (UX) writer, content designer, or content strategist. Indeed, in this new age of content, where words and content strategies play a central role in software and service design, there are many descriptions for what writers do. Whatever your title, your job is probably to persuade someone to do something, inform them how to do it, or both.

You also may be responsible for the relationship your product or service has with your customers. Doing it well requires you to understand the difference between your character and its voice and tone.

Character covers everything you do with your designs, including content. It is an expression of your company's core values and attributes as defined by a *marketing strategy*. It captures the essence of who you are and how you want your brand to be perceived by current and prospective customers alike. Look to your brand's character to maintain consistency and alignment across touchpoints.

Your character has a voice, just like the voice of a character in a novel, movie, or video game. Your character's voice is the expression of your brand through written content, face-to-face interactions, and any other interaction with customers. Through both voice and tone, you can modify who that character becomes—I call this a *flex*—but your voice needs to remain consistent with your brand.

Why is that important? Because an erratic character fractured by an inconsistent voice can erode the relationship you are trying to build with your audience. Customers need to feel secure. They need to count on you like a trusted friend or family member. The building and maintaining of trust comes from a consistent character, and that includes how that character talks.

Imagine this. You've found a new butcher shop, and over repeated visits you've made a connection with the butcher. He's been professional, inquisitive, and knowledgeable. He always asks what's important to you and listens to your needs. Then one day you walk in and have a different experience. He's bombastically joking around with everyone, doesn't pay you much attention, and then talks down to you by insisting you buy something other than what you asked for. Any trust you had built with him previously is probably gone at that point. You're uncertain why he treated you differently than you expected. It made you feel uncomfortable.

Now, you don't expect anyone to be slavishly consistent. We tolerate and understand variations, or *flexes*, in a person's behavior. Maybe he's just in a bad mood today. But a dramatic change in voice might drive you to leave and never come back. This is why consistency of character, brought to life through a consistent voice, is key to any successful *brand strategy*.

Character is part of any successful brand strategy, which usually starts with a company or product vision followed by things like brand purpose and brand promise.[1] Character is defined by a description and a set of attributes. Coming up with the right character takes exploration, customer research, iteration, and development. Let's start by getting clear on the role of character in the hierarchy of character, voice and tone.

---

[1] The details of brand strategy are beyond the scope of this book. For a good introduction to the topic, I recommend *Building Strong Brands*[1] by David Aaker.

Character	Character is an expression of core values and attributes. It captures who you are and how you want your brand to be perceived by current and prospective customers. All communications should reinforce character.

Example: The character of Zappos, the online shoe retailer, includes a core value that tells employees to "create fun and a little weirdness."[2] Their voice reinforces the idea that "we are playful and fun." |
| Voice | Voice is a reflection of character. It's the relationship you create with customers through written content and in-person interactions. It's who you are, how you show up, and what you believe. You can flex voice to meet customer needs across touchpoints, but your voice needs to remain consistent with your character.

Example: When you order with Zappos they express their quirky, fun nature both in on-screen content and in-person interactions. When you call, they might reinforce their voice by asking how you're doing and relating a funny anecdote or an insightful observation. |
| Tone | While voice is a reflection of character, tone is about mood. Flex tone based on in-the-moment situations. It's how you feel right now or the emotion you tap into. Context and timing are key to successfully flexing tone. For example, you wouldn't be lighthearted if you're asking people to do something difficult.

Example: If you need to return something, the Zappos voice might momentarily shift from fun and weird to serious and helpful. |

---

[2] https://www.zappos.com/about/what-we-live-by

Keeping a consistent voice is important, but you have more flexibility with tone. Voice and tone play different roles. Your character comes to life through its voice. But what about emotion? That's where tone comes through. No character, whether real or fictitious, seems human without it.

Tone taps into emotion in ways that character and voice cannot. As Kristina Adams so eloquently put it, "tone is your mood"[2]. But mood fluctuates. How you feel changes—sometimes dramatically—from moment to moment. Flexing your tone allows you to make essential adjustments in how you sound when you are celebrating success versus times when you are apologizing for making a mistake. If you create a certain mood by flexing your tone to celebrate a success or apologize for an error, that will likely change shortly after you move on. It's highly contextual. Tone doesn't always deepen relationships, but it can help us express appropriate emotions and make our interactions with customers desirable and memorable. Strategic use of tone can enhance engagement.

Mistakes happen. A momentary hiccup in the experience opens the door for you to consider using humor. Responding to a mistake with humor can strengthen your relationship or damage it. What comes before and after informs the flex in tone. If this interruption occurred in the middle of a critical task, humor could damage the relationship, not strengthen it. Again, context and timing are key to flexing tone. I talk more flexing voice and tone in Chapter 6.

Where voice and tone live in a content strategy

Whatever framework you use for your broader content strategy, your strategy for voice and tone will live in the center of it.

Kristina Halvorson, CEO at content strategy agency Brain Traffic, defines content strategy this way: "Content strategy guides the creation, delivery, and governance of useful, usable content"[16]. In general, content strategists follow a traditional strategic model: they discover what needs to be done, figure out how to do it, execute on it, manage it, and maintain it.

Halvorson is not alone. While at Amazon, content strategist Carol Valdez developed what she calls the three S's: Substance, Structure, and Speaker:

Substance
: WHAT you say. It's the subject matter, as defined by what you discovered about your audience, and what has the potential to resonate with their needs.

Structure
: HOW you deliver content. It's how you make sense out of it, make it consistent, and make it consumable. Structure is often supported by things like style and grammar guides.

Speaker
: WHO you become through your voice. It's your character brought to life through how you talk, a character that comes across as relevant and human.

"I've always felt that content is a bit like an iceberg," she says. "People see the limited text that appears in an interface, but don't realize the careful work that goes into making that content effective. I wanted to find a way to break down what goes into crafting content, and make that creative process more visible to everyone."

That's what I'm focusing on when I talk about voice and tone strategy: becoming a speaker, a character who connects with customers through voice. Substance and structure are part of the overall strategic framework, but defining the speaker—your character's voice—requires a framework of its own within the larger content strategy.

Marketing and product voice

You may be a copywriter working on landing pages for a website. Or a UX writer crafting microcopy for a mobile app. Or perhaps you're writing help articles for an online retailer. When it comes to voice and tone, regardless of your job title, your goal should be the same: connect with your customers and build a relationship. Relationships that create connections are relationships that work.

Marketing voice and product voice are connected like a married couple who are different in their own ways but rely on each other for success.

Product voice informs and marketing voice persuades. But unlike the world of advertising portrayed by Don Draper in the TV show *Man Men*, where copywriters executed solely on a separate strategy for brand voice, today's marketing and product content writers and strategists are finding ways to work together. If the teams of writers in your organization are siloed, it's time to break down those walls and encourage collaboration.

Marketing voice doesn't just have to get people in the door. It must also engage them with the promise of meaning that is delivered with the product voice. Your product's voice—the voice of the character inside the product experience—builds and evolves the relationship started by the persuasive efforts of the marketing team. To deliver consistently exceptional customer experiences, focus on the development of a single end-to-end strategy that covers all of the touchpoints throughout the customer journey. That can be far more effective than several strategies covering different parts of the experience.

The online retailer Trunk Club's website,[3] or *front door*, portrays a character that is all about personalized service and a unique approach to styling, with benefits such as convenience and simplicity—things meant to persuade you to use their service. Once you start using their service, the voice and tone shifts from persuasion to something more empowering and aspirational. You feel like the product experience is delivering on the promises made at the front door. The voice doesn't change, it builds and evolves, just like a relationship with a real human might.

The importance of relationships

Relationships are connections. Connections aren't always based on polite and friendly experiences. Customers can find meaning and establish connection even in situations in which they are treated rudely.

The Soup Nazi character from NBC TV's Seinfeld made really great soup. His soup was so remarkable that soup lovers would endure long wait times and the disdain of the chef just to get a cup. The Soup Nazi forced his patrons to queue up in a perfectly straight line and yelled at them if they said

---

[3] https://www.trunkclub.com/

anything to him other than which soup they wanted. "No soup for you," was the punishment for dissent.

Did customers who returned to the soup shop daily do so just because it was the best soup in town? Or, was it because they understood and enjoyed the experience? Was it the fragile relationship between the chef and his patrons or was it about his customers wanting to be part of the in-crowd—the patrons lucky enough to survive the gauntlet, follow the rules, and receive the reward: a piping hot bowl of the chef's daily taste sensation.

The Seinfeld characters loved the Soup Nazi because—through his voice—he set a customer expectation that the experience would be the same every time. While brash and mildly abusive, The Soup Nazi was passionate, unabashedly authentic, and believable. He also made amazingly tasty soups. The experience he provided meant something to those who braved the lunch counter line in the quest for a perfect chowder or stew. He connected with them in a way they desired.

I'm not suggesting you be rude to your customers. My point is that marketing voice is usually about enticing people to experience something by promising that their effort will be rewarded with something of meaning. Product voice is about delivering on those promises. In a perfect world, marketing voice and product voice should work together.

A solid voice and tone strategy addresses customer needs, identifies character attributes and principles, and provides examples along with clear guidance on how to flex your voice and tone appropriately.

CHAPTER 2
A Simple Framework for Voice and Tone

Careers in content strategy can lead to great things, exciting challenges, and the power to create positive change for both your company and your customers. That's been true for me, especially when I was given the lead content strategy role on a huge design team, responsible for the quality and effectiveness of all our content across a suite of websites and products.

In no time at all, the head of design came to me and emphatically said, "our competitors are nipping at our heels. We need to shake things up, get our designs out of a rut, and start creating content that can clearly help us win the game now and in the future."

Up until that point, my teams and I had been doing a great job at executing on an existing strategy, even beefing it up with some new principles and examples. But now I was being asked to change the game, to entirely reimagine how we connected and talked to our customers through all of our content. I was given no clear goal to guide my teams through this, and I wasn't sure exactly what we were being asked to deliver. But whatever it was, I would be responsible for bringing the organization along on the journey.

I learned a lot from the experience, including the value of reaching outside our organization to get new ideas and coaching from people who were not currently committed to our existing strategy or even in our industry. I also learned about the value of storytelling in crafting a winning strategy and the need to develop separate frameworks for flexing your voice and tone, both of which I'll explore later in this book.

With our strategy in hand, I was asked by other teams to help them develop their own plans of attack. To do so, I borrowed lessons learned from companies I had helped in the past that had faced similar challenges.

Out of all these experiences I developed the Vertical Voice and Tone Framework. It's a simplified approach to devising a voice and tone strategy. It has proved to be instrumental in helping several teams participate in, and even champion, their own strategies.

Instead of following a linear design process, such as the Double Diamond,[1] this framework represents a vertical process that you can repeat as you learn and adjust to changes, a process located somewhere in the middle of any broader double diamond your design team might be following.

I took what needs to be included in any successful voice and tone strategy and boiled it down to the four basic building blocks—driven by a goal. Because the goal is the high-level target, I built this set of blocks down from there, rather than up from the bottom. Figure 2.1 outlines the framework. Starting with these basic building blocks can help you lead your team to a positive outcome.

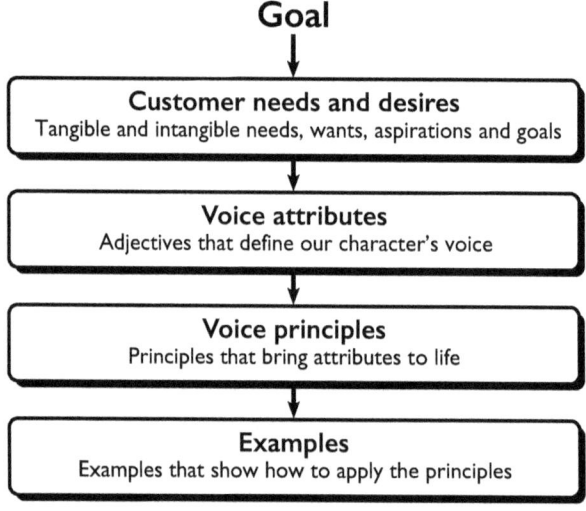

Figure 2.1 – Vertical Voice and Tone Framework

---

[1] If you are not familiar with the Double Diamond, this article by Design Council is a good place to start: "What is the framework for innovation? Design Council's evolved Double Diamond"[12].

This basic framework does not include front-end discovery efforts, such as *customer research* and development of *personas*. It also doesn't include things that live in the delivery phase, such as guidelines for structure and style, which I talk about in Chapter 9. This framework focuses on voice and tone and how to develop a strategy within your larger content strategy or design process.

Start by setting a goal for your voice and tone

Start with a high-level yet achievable goal for your voice and tone. This is your target: what you are aiming for by employing the framework. Making sure you have a goal, one that has the buy-in of everyone on your design team, will also mitigate churn around specific language and words down the road. With a clear goal, you can always ask, "is this word or phrase in service to our goal?" If not, move on.

Here's some guidance on setting a goal:

- Get the input of key stakeholders, especially marketing managers and design leads
- Research trends and incorporate them into your goal
- Align with your company's vision and business and marketing goals
- Tie-in to something aspirational that can resonate with your customers

Often the impetus for creating a new strategy for voice and tone comes from management making one of the following cases for change:

- "If we don't do something like this our competitors will."
- "Our customers are getting something from our competitors that we're not delivering. We not only need to catch up, we need to offer something more."

In the first case, you're getting out in front of disruption, in the second you're catching up. Getting out in front is the more strategic approach, and it creates the most compelling story for getting buy-in from stakeholders and leadership.

Figure 2.2 – Identifying goals

At TurboTax, we adopted the first approach, and we made it clear to leadership how voice and tone could protect our competitive advantage. Faced with the threat of powerful science-based "magic" from growing data giants like Google and Facebook, we argued that the meaning delivered by voice and tone would be our secret sauce. Sure, they had the potential to wield their wizardry and deliver a seemingly magical new way of doing taxes, but we'd always be ahead of them with relationships that delivered what customers really wanted: meaningful connections. We knew our customers wanted this, and we were confident it would serve to build positive word of mouth and brand loyalty.

> We set a goal that focused on emotion: "Go beyond ease and accuracy to create emotional engagement with our customers."

In this case, we didn't abandon the strategic pillars that continued to be important and necessary for our product—ease and accuracy. Rather, we added a third one: emotional engagement. This was based on a strong case for change: If we don't connect with emotional needs, someone else will.

But in creating a goal centered on emotion we also considered trends in the world of software as a service and how those trends influence customer expectations, something you will want to consider when crafting a goal for your voice and tone efforts. We knew that emotional design[2] was and continues to be an emerging trend to the point that customers now expect it. And like a perceptive friend who senses an emotional need, the voice of our character can meet and even exceed those expectations, including eliciting emotional connections between your customer experience and your customers.

Think about emotion as a new and important zone on your playing field when crafting your goal. Depending on your industry and competitive landscape, you might come up with something like "Deliver on their needs while turning their negative feelings about our service into positive ones," or "Take the conversation beyond actions and tasks to include successes and aspirations." Both of these can respect existing pillars of strategy while adding a new one that focuses on emotional needs.

Building block #1: Customer needs and desires

Once you have a high-level, clear goal for your voice and tone, you can start developing how your team will achieve that goal. This starts with the customer. By the time you're applying this framework, the broader design team should have already conducted research and defined customer personas. Use that research as a starting point to decide which customer needs you should focus on to connect with voice and tone.

As an outgrowth of your research, everything you do stems from the customer needs you identify in the early stages of your strategy development. Just putting a list of those needs in your voice and tone strategy can change the game by identifying needs that may not yet be well defined.

---

[2] Interaction Design Foundation, "What is Emotional Design?"[17].

> **What about customer personas?**
>
> Design and product management teams like to create personas. While they can be helpful, they often rely too heavily on one or two customer types rather than focusing on more universal needs and desires. And they don't always tell you much about customer behaviors, which are the windows into what customers actually want.
>
> Here's a typical customer persona that focuses on characteristics but doesn't tell you how this person might behave:
>
> **Meghan Smith, female, 28:**
>
> - Married with two children
> - Nurse
> - Homeowner
> - Has a smartphone
> - Saving for retirement

For your basic voice and tone framework leave things like customer personas to the broader design team and instead create two crisp and narrow lists: One for customer needs and one for desires. The mere presence of these lists helps to keep everyone on track—designers, marketers, product managers, and senior leaders—as you develop your character's voice.

As I work through strategic opportunities in this book, I'll be exploring tangible and intangible needs, things that speak to the transactional and the aspirational nature of the relationships you intend to create. When you reach for intangible, emotional desires you're truly being strategic.

But intangible needs aren't always revealed through traditional research methods, including user testing and data analytics. It's acceptable and worthwhile to draw from your own experience and expertise. With customer insights from both your research and data from outside sources, such as books and other research, you and your team can ask, what problems are our customers facing? What are they feeling? What do they aspire to do or become?

To create your two short lists of customer needs and desires, take the information at your disposal, and then go broad then narrow in on things that are either transactional or emotional. I'll talk more later about picking needs that can be met with the relationship you want to create, not science and data. But to give you some idea of what I'm talking about, "I need you to import the information from my insurance carrier" is a need that's met by science. "I need you to help me understand this information" is a need that's met by voice. Figure 2.3 shows a typical list of needs and desires and Figure 2.4 shows an example of the list we created at TurboTax.

Needs (tangible)	Desires (intangible)
1. Pick a product 2. Get signed in 3. Accomplish the task 4. Enter my info	1. Feel safe and secure 2. Feel smart 3. Be treated like an adult 4. Turn negative emotions into positive

Figure 2.3 – List of needs and desires

The TurboTax Customer	
Needs (tangible)	Desires (intangible)
1. Feel confident they can do it 2. Know it's done right 3. Get their biggest tax refund	1. To do their taxes their way 2. To feel good about their money 3. To succeed (be a hero!)

Figure 2.4 – Example: TurboTax

16   A Simple Framework for Voice and Tone

Building block #2: Voice attributes

Once you've narrowed to a set of needs and desires that are worth pursuing—a set that gives you the opportunity to be strategic—you can ask your team, "who do we need to become to meet those needs?" More importantly, "how will our character talk to people in a way that connects with what they need and want?"

You should be looking to create a list of three-to-five attributes that describe your voice. An attribute is an adjective that defines who you are when you're talking to customers. The old adage "less is more" applies here. If you can keep the list to three, it will be more useful to writers. These attributes must play in concert with your overall brand attributes. Sometimes they're the same, but often it's more strategic to create a subset of attributes that are about voice. This book explores the latter approach.

Figure 2.5 – Sweetgreen advertisement

An accurate voice attribute for the ad in Figure 2.5 might be "enthusiastic." That's an attribute that is clearly expressed through voice. Your goal is to create a voice that gets your customers to come back to you with a description of your content that relays the idea of sounding enthusiastic. If they describe you as "energetic," "peppy," or "spirited," all synonyms that track to your goal of sounding enthusiastic, you know you're connecting. Your strategy is working.

Again, the more strategic opportunity lies within desire. You need to deliver on basic needs. But when you connect with aspirations, you're no longer just like everyone else.

Creating attributes through role models

Think of someone in your life with whom you share a strong bond, someone who usually leaves you feeling happy and energized. It could be a family member, close friend, or a mentor. When they're helping you, coaching you, or sharing some advice, how do they sound? What adjectives would you use to describe their voice? There's a good chance they're lifting you up with what they say and how they say it, not just helping you with something tangible.

Now think about how you would describe their character. Are they a "smart friend," or "wise elder"? This also is key to how you connect with people through voice. It's usually something defined by brand strategy, but it also informs the attributes you might use to describe your voice.

Guardrails

Putting some guardrails around your voice attributes is yet another method that can make your strategy even more useful. Let's say "perceptive" is an attribute that describes your voice. You can make that crystal clear by saying you're "perceptive, but not nosey." It's a "this, but not that" approach that further defines who you are and makes the target clear for writers.

It can be helpful to provide a description for each attribute. This is a 2-3 sentence paragraph, like the following:

> **Perceptive, but not nosey:** We know what customers want even before they know it themselves. We understand them, and we show up with relevant options and answers.

Building block #3: Principles for voice

The most useful, tool-like part of any design strategy is a set of principles. These guide you and help you bring your voice attributes to life. Principles are specific and targeted. And they represent what you believe is important.

Microsoft has a set of principles they use for their brand voice. Here is one that is particularly specific and targeted:

> **Ready to lend a hand:** We show customers we're on their side. We anticipate their real needs and offer great information at just the right time.
> —Microsoft, "Microsoft's brand voice: Above all, simple and human"[22]

A bit of confusion for some can be the difference between an attribute and a principle. When crafting a principle, be sure it's about the *how* and not the *who*. "Inspiring" is an example of an attribute. It's the adjective your design team might use to describe who you are when you connect with customers. "Talk about the possibilities" is a principle that can bring "inspiring" to life through voice. It's one specific way you might do it.

Microsoft confuses these a bit in their set of principles. In the same list as "Ready to lend a hand" they have a principle identified as "Warm and relaxed," which is more a set of attributes than a specific principle for how to talk. It might better to turn "Warm and relaxed" into an action that brings it to life, perhaps "Speak softly and calmly."

Another misconception is that a set of principles is all-or-nothing. You'll often hear non-designers, such as marketing or product managers, say something like, "I thought we were supposed to be perceptive. I don't get that in this copy."

That's because a set of principles represents a range of options. They're not a unified block. Just like the fluidity in any casual conversation you might have with a good friend, there is some overlap. At any point in the experience, depending what the customer needs at that moment, you might apply one or two of your principles within a single line of copy on a screen or in the conversation you're having throughout a broader touchpoint. As long as you're making a meaningful connection and building the relationship in line with your strategy, you're on track, regardless of which or how many principles are in play.

Principles can range from those that feed a transactional relationship all the way to ones that speak to hopes and dreams. Just like attributes, it's most useful to put forth three to five, and to keep the descriptions for them to two, maybe three, sentences. Here are some examples from TurboTax:

- **Transactional principle:** Assure them it's accurate
- **Aspirational principle:** Speak to their higher self

Building block #4: Examples

The most important part of communicating your voice and tone strategy is the set of examples you include. These can be existing examples that show your strategy at work, or they can be mock-ups that show the possibilities of a new strategy.

I've taken many new voice and tone strategies on road shows to skeptical audiences that include marketing teams, development managers, product owners, and executives responsible for profit and loss. As I walk through attributes and principles, I see wrinkled brows and tilting heads. But when I get to the examples, eyes light up and heads start to nod.

It may seem obvious, but I can't stress enough the importance of carving out time to curate and/or create the best examples possible. They not only create understanding and advocacy for your strategy, they allow your writers to stress test the principles and practice bringing your voice and tone to life. In Chapter 6, I talk about the importance of spending time with your content teams to brainstorm examples for each principle and also creating examples that illustrate the overlap and interplay of a combination of principles.

One powerful presentation tactic is the "from-to." Find existing content that clearly shows the absence of your new strategy, re-write it to show the possibilities, and then put them together on a slide, or one after the other on two slides (see Figure 2.6).

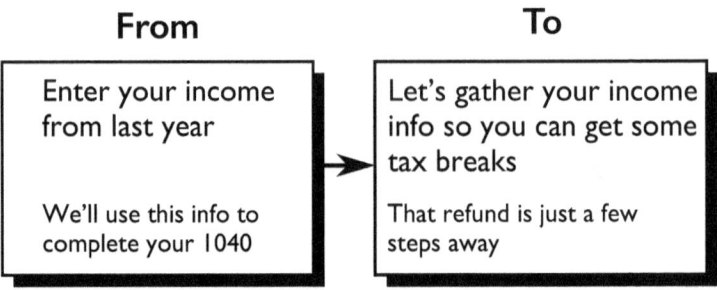

Figure 2.6 – From-to presentation example

Similar to the "this, not that" approach, examples tied to individual attributes or principles can also be presented in a list of "it sounds like this" and "it doesn't sound like this" content snippets. If you're trying to catch up with a competitor, it can be useful to include outside examples that show how their voice contrasts with yours.

Now that I've walked you through the basics of the Vertical Voice and Tone Framework, let's dive deeper into each of the basic building blocks.

CHAPTER 3
Building Block 1: Needs and Desires (but mostly desires)

Building block 1 identifies and documents customer needs and desires. Customer desires, not just needs, are the key to a winning voice and tone strategy. "I need to sign in" is a basic, tangible need. "I want to feel safe and secure" is more of a desire. In this chapter I dig deeper into this foundational building block. That includes revisiting the value and importance of a clear goal. I also tie in the role that storytelling plays in figuring out what your customer really needs and wants.

Vision and goal

A vision, followed by a goal, leads to customer desires. A good vision is one that seems impossible to achieve. You might create one just for your voice and tone or leverage the one set by your company. Either way, it should generate creative tension between what you imagine the future could look like and what is possible now. That valuable tension can drive your team to be more innovative, including in their content. As Alison E. Berman eloquently illustrates in a recent article on SingularityHub,[1] it has the "power to motivate."

The vision informs the goal I illustrated in Chapter 2. It's not necessary to include the vision in your strategy document. The goal is the target. It's meant to be achievable in the near term, whereas the vision is more about what you can imagine down a longer road. The goal should be lofty too, but it should also make sense in the context of what your content team is trying to do. Ask your team, "what's the prize?" What would make your product or service stand apart from your competitors using voice and tone? What, if you achieved it, would have your customers saying, "I love you?"

---

[1] Berman, Alison E., "The Motivating Power of a Massive Transformative Purpose"[6].

You can't really narrow to an actionable set of customer needs and desires without a clear goal for your voice and tone. Writers need to know what they're shooting for before they can craft content that addresses specific needs. Here is an example that a health insurance company might use:

- **Product vision:** Change the health insurance landscape from one of limited coverage to a world of endless choices
- **Goal for voice:** Go beyond just talking about securing and paying for insurance to planning for a healthier future

If you're not sure what your goal should be, ask for help. Brainstorm with your research team or marketing leaders. Go outside your company and seek provocation, coaching, and advice[2] from people who have faced similar challenges and figured them out. Ideally you want people who are already winning the game in industries that are analogous to, but not the same as, your product or service.

Desires are the most important strategic target

Desire is what makes us human, and it has much more to do with emotion than everyday needs. Today, you may need to go to the store. That's a basic need to get something to eat. And if someone told you the best route to the store and how to find a parking spot, you would probably find that information valuable. If they say it clearly and concisely, all the better.

Tasks need to get done, and content designers and UX writers help people complete tasks. But it doesn't have to stop there. By also tapping into your customers' desires—their wants, their hopes and dreams—you can take your strategy to a higher level and gain a competitive advantage.

"We want to move toward desires because that's how real people are," says Wendy Castleman, veteran design researcher and founder of DeveloPeople UX, a firm that helps a company and leaders use innovative methods to succeed. "We hate the Department of Motor Vehicles. But we love that one guy at the DMV who makes the whole experience seem OK by telling us,

---

[2] Caldwell, John. "Provocation Can Lead to Emotional Design"[7].

'yes, this is painful, but it's all going to be over in 10 minutes.' He taps into our emotion, our desire to leave."

I've lost count the number of times a design lead or a product manager has said something like, "shouldn't our content demystify the complex or guide them through the task? Isn't content design about taking jargon and turning it into plain English?"

"Yes," I say. "Absolutely. We always do that. And so do our competitors. That's why we also need to elevate our strategic thinking to differentiate our voice and our experience, and we also need to talk about meeting customer desires through voice and tone."

"We want to become a human-like character that our customers want to know," I'll continue, "that person who challenges them to pursue their dreams. To do that, we must do more than just demystify things. We must talk about possibilities."

The fashion brand Chanel has a voice that clearly taps into the desire of their customers to live an elevated existence (see Figure 3.1). Through their voice, they basically say, "This is an exclusive brand for sophisticated people." It works for them.

Figure 3.1 – Ad for Chanel Paris-Riviera

But what about those customers who don't care about aspirational things? Some just want you to stay out of their way with any aspirational content. Emotional engagement needs to be optional. You need to resonate with the story they are telling themselves about what is going to happen in your website or product.

Many video games do this with great success, especially those with a narrative format, like *The Elder Scrolls* or *Bioshock*. They offer players the option to learn and engage in the story, but players are always in control of their destiny and completely free to follow their own desire and do what they want in the game.

Google's "I'm Feeling Lucky" button is a simple example of optional engagement (see Figure 3.2). The regular search gives users all the options, including some elevated content that attempts to tap into what they really want. The "I'm Feeling Lucky" button offers a path to complete the task with as little engagement as possible.

Building Block 1: Needs and Desires (but mostly desires)   25

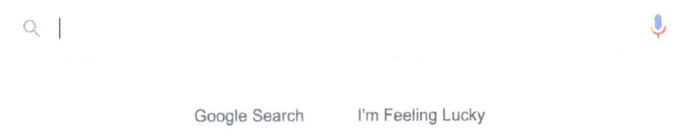

Figure 3.2 – Google "I'm Feeling Lucky" search

When people are open to engagement and growth, it's an opportunity for you and your strategy. Moo.com has done this well. Their bread and butter is business cards, fliers, and other materials for small businesses, but they also offer valuable info on succeeding as an entrepreneur. No one really wants a lesson when they're ordering business cards, so they make it enticing and let people discover it for themselves. In addition to ordering materials, their website has inviting links labeled "Inspiration" and "Business tips" (see Figure 3.3). It's optional, but a lot of people engage with it. That result: happy customers who often say they "love Moo!"

Figure 3.3 – Moo "Get Inspired" page

Using storytelling to discover customer desires

You may already have a wealth of customer data and surprising customer insights from in-house research. But it's a good idea for your content team to augment that with some deep customer empathy of your own. Storytelling, with its age-old rules and techniques, is one powerful way to discover what your customer desires. I talk about the power of story at the end of this book and then go deeper into it in an article on TheContent-

Wrangler.com. Creating a narrative for your customer's story can lead to deep customer empathy, uncovering what's most important to your customer as they face their biggest challenges or deepest fears.

I once took a memorable storytelling workshop facilitated by an innovator named Greg Ames at Proctor & Gamble. He told us a story about their company's efforts to break into the laundry detergent market in Latin America. Their initial approach was to persuade customers that Tide laundry detergent would make their lives easier: Use our product, and you'll spend less time washing dirty clothes. That was the company's story, complete with a marketing plan and clearly defined "reasons to believe." But it wasn't working. So, they found their ideal customer, learned everything they could about her, and then crafted her story using the plot-driven narrative circle outlined in Joseph Campbell's influential book, *The Hero with a Thousand Faces*[10].

In Campbell's narrative, there's an all-important threshold in which the hero of the story (your customer) "enters the cave," which is where they face their deepest fears, discover what they most fear losing, and then push through it. This is where the hero must be willing to cross over a point of no return in order to emerge victorious. The P&G team discovered their customer's biggest fear was losing the love of her family. And washing their clothes was one important way in which she believed she secured that love every day. By diminishing the task of washing clothes, they were essentially diminishing what was most important to her.

This changed things for their marketing and product teams, and their writers. Their customer's character went from something like "efficient homemaker" to "deeply loving matriarch." And that changed how they talked to those customers, the benefit they focused on with their voice and tone. Ames didn't reveal what they landed on, but it's reasonable to assume that they went from something like "Spend more time with your family, and less time doing laundry" to "Every stitch of clothing you wash for your family will be fresh and bright."

Building a list of customer needs and desires

By listening to and understanding your customers, whether through storytelling or other means, you'll gain the insights required to put together an initial list of customer needs and desires that can be met through voice and tone:

- A basic need is *tangible*. It must be met to move forward. The customer can't or won't use your product or service unless you meet that need. For example, a rider calling a car from Uber needs to know where the car is and how long it will take to arrive. They don't *need* that car to do anything but get them from here to there.
- An emotional desire is *intangible*. It doesn't have to be met to move forward. The customer can use your product without, necessarily, feeling safe. But when you meet that emotional need, their engagement with you and your service becomes more meaningful. It seems human, and customers are more likely to move forward with confidence. For example, an Uber rider may want to be treated like a friend by the driver. This is a desire, not a need, but if the driver is friendly, then the rider may be more likely to recommend Uber to friends.

Start with a list of basic, tangible needs. Comb through your customer learnings and insights. With voice and tone in mind, select needs that your voice must meet for the customer to move forward or get a task done, writing them in the customer's voice.

Go broad. Brainstorm with your team and get everything out and on paper or a white board. Don't limit yourself. At this point, there are no bad ideas about what's most important to include.

Depending on your product, service, or website, a working list of basic needs might look like the following, though it will likely be much longer:

Basic needs (things that are tangible)

- I need you to speak my language
- I need you to guide me through each task
- I need you to explain things in detail
- I need you to know when I'm stuck
- I need to fully understand what you're telling me
- I need you to stay out of my way when I'm concentrating
- I need you to keep me on the right path
- I need to fail gracefully if I don't use this correctly
- I need to maintain control
- I need to know I can trust you

Some of these may delve into emotion. But they're still basic needs. To distinguish a basic need from desire, ask yourself if it is a necessity or an "awesome to have." Tangible needs are more of a necessity.

It may not always be clear. That's the nature of crafting a customer-backed strategic approach. Not everything is black or white. You're dealing with a lot of grey and a lot of overlap, and that's OK. The important thing is to identify a set of basic needs you must always meet. Then, you can start to identify a list of desires that represents a next-level strategic opportunity.

Once you have a broad list of needs, go broad on desires. Look for things that are emotional, things that speak to human-like relationships. A broad list of desires might look like the following:

Emotional desires (intangible)

- I want to feel like you're always with me
- I want you to care about me
- I want you to treat me like I'm smart, like I'm an adult
- I want to feel like I can master this thing
- I want to define what success looks like for me
- I want to feel connected to others facing the same challenge

- I want you to recognize I have a sense of purpose
- I want you to understand that I might be feeling vulnerable
- I want to learn something new
- I want to get something more than just the answer to my question

A lot of this stems from what your customers believe. You need to tease out what you think they believe from their actions and words. This requires a bit of inference based on what they actually say and do.

Castleman offers the following example, starting with the customer saying, "I believe I'm not good at math, so I'm not going to be good at this." Actually, according to Castleman, "The stated need may in fact be, 'I need to know that math won't get in the way.' Desire is more than that. It's about getting to an aspirational place where you declare, 'I want to feel OK that the math thing doesn't really matter.'"

Validate what you think you know

Everything I'm talking about in this book has to do with connecting with people through human-sounding content. Putting together lists of needs and desires is foundational to that. And while it's possible for writers and strategists to do this without actually talking directly to people, doing so helps tremendously.

Before you start to narrow your list of needs and desires, ask yourself, how can I be sure that the desires I teased out as possible targets for voice and tone will resonate with my customer's story?

"If you're the receiver of research findings from someone else, you tend to interpret that research based on your own beliefs," Castleman says. "That's what we call *confirmation bias*. We ignore those things that conflict with what we believe to be true."

To mitigate that, it's a good design practice for your content team, no matter how big or how small, to go out and do their own research. When you create a new strategy for voice and tone, doing your own research should be a critical and recurring step to test what you think you know.

I'm talking about everything from ambushing people on the street to recruiting a few folks to come to your design studio and chat with you.

Don't get caught up in the need for rigorous research methodology. Many groundbreaking products and voice and tone strategies have been created by meeting random customers in coffee shops and showing them simple drawings or words on a page. Take your list of needs and desires and create some down and dirty, *content-first prototypes*. One way to do this is to create a set of printed *wireframes* that illustrate a piece of the experience (see Figure 3.4 for an example of such a wireframe).

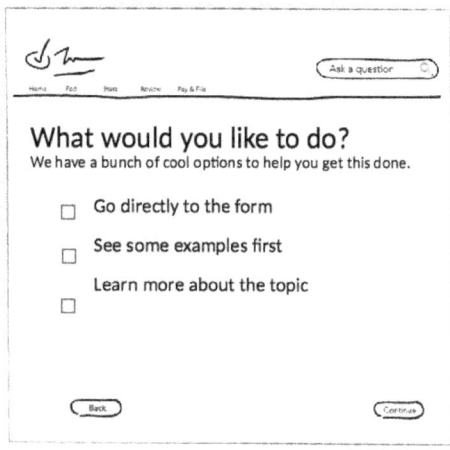

Figure 3.4 – Content-first wireframe

You can also just have a conversation with your customers. Present them with some problem statements that illustrate the customer needs and desires you want to test. Have a list of questions ready that target what you hope to learn. Ask why after every answer. Look for surprises in the customer's answers and ask yourself how they might challenge your thinking. All of this will help you validate and refine your lists.

"No matter what you do, you should be listening for the actual words that describe what you're thinking about writing (your voice and tone)," Castleman says. "It doesn't need to be their voice and tone, but it needs to connect to it."

Narrow to the best opportunities for voice

The final lists you create for this building block should be uncomfortably narrow. That's what makes innovation possible. If you stay too broad, your strategy will end up being too broad to connect, too watered down to have any real meaning. At this point, you may need to dig deep and find the confidence to move forward with something that causes a little voice inside your head to nag at you, asking, "did we get this right?" That's actually a good thing. Your odds of success are far better by moving forward with something narrow.

Start with your list of tangible needs. Pare it down to no more than four or five. Your list only needs to represent the kinds of things you will always address, not the entirety of your customer's basic needs. Give the short list some breadth. No one need should be similar to another.

Then move on to emotional desires. "Emotions are things you would actually feel," Castleman says, "things like fear, excitement, or upset. If you don't have an emotion word in your description of a desire, you may not be looking at an actual desire."

Your goal should be a list of no more than five desires that focus on what your voice and tone strategy can deliver. As you look to narrow your broader list, ask yourself, can the way you talk to people address this desire? Is voice and tone the only way your design team can connect with this desire?

At Intuit, we used a technique called 2x2 narrowing.[3] With this technique, you select two criteria to drive the process. For example, you might choose "possibility" and "convenience" as your driving criteria. You plot those on a two-axis graph (see Figure 3.5). You then look at each desire and assign it a place in the graph based on whether it speaks strongly to each criterion or not.

---

[3] Intuit has posted information on 2x2 narrowing on SlideShare ("2x2 Narrowing"[18]) and Vimeo ("2x2 Method for Narrowing"[4]).

For example, "I want to become financially independent" is a desire that speaks strongly to possibility, but not so strongly to convenience. On the other hand, "I want to complete my taxes quickly" speaks strongly to convenience, but not so strongly to possibility.

Whether you use 2x2 narrowing or some other technique, your objective is to identify which desires match your most important criteria and then select a list of four to five focused desires.

Declare your own desires in the relationship

Creating a human-like relationship with your customers also means you need to show up. You're a character in their story. That means more than just describing your character with distinct adjectives. It means declaring your own desires in the relationship. In a real relationship between two people, each person has something at stake.

Your customer might want to feel like you care about them. That's an intangible desire. And you might want them to know that you care about them. That, too, is an intangible desire. It's your desire in the relationship, a desire that can be expressed through voice and tone.

Create a third list, one that focuses on the emotional desires your character wants to have met in the relationship with your customers. Depending on your product, service, or website, it could look something like this:

Your character's intangible desires

- I want to help our customers succeed
- I want to inspire the customer to feel confident
- I want to be their go-to source for information
- I want to create a safe place for the exchange of info
- I want to turn their negative feelings into positive ones

As you can see, these may not be as explicitly emotional. They may also seem like you're just mirroring what the customer wants. That's OK. Don't get too caught up in making this particular list something groundbreaking or innovative. Simply writing down some of your own character desires and putting them on a page next to your customer's needs and desires has the power to humanize the relationship you want to create with voice and tone. This is all about your character showing up when speaking to the customer. Coach your writers to look for the right moments, some key opportunities, to express your character's wants in line with its attributes and principles. Keep your list short.

"Even if you're just writing a conversation, knowing where you're coming from is important to the customer," Castleman says. "Customers will assume you're trying to get something from them, so they'll come to you wanting to give away as little as possible. But if you make it clear that you're not just trying to take them for a ride, it changes their mindset. They might connect with you, decide for themselves they should be open to you."

Understand human nature, not just characteristics

As you are narrowing your list of customer needs and desires, remember that customer personas can help, but you need to go beyond personas. Personas can promote group think and lead you to focus on characteristics instead of behaviors.

It's important that you "deeply know your audience," says cognitive neuroscientist, Dr. Carmen Simon, founder of Memzy, an agency that helps organizations use brain science to create and deliver memorable content experiences. "People tend to pay more attention to what needs to be solved in the immediate future and to what is immediately relevant," she says in an article for The Content Wrangler[29]. "The brain system responsible for focusing attention on what counts and ignoring everything else is called the Reticular Activating System (RAS). People are acutely interested in themselves, so when your content offers solutions to personal, nagging issues, their RAS lets you in, regardless of information overload. The old adage 'know your audience' needs an update to 'deeply know your audience.' The better you use their profile (likes, dislikes, immediate needs and goals), the longer you can keep them paying attention."

It's also true that all humans are a bit crazy. This is at the heart of *cognitive science* and emotional design, and it should be top of mind for any strategist trying to figure out how to connect with people through voice and tone.

Understanding the craziness of humans can help you stress test your lists of needs and desires. It can also help you when it's time to figure out how to communicate a well-rounded rationale to stakeholders. What I mean by crazy is that most people think with their emotional brains first, and their rational brains last. If you want people to choose your product experience, even rave about it, and if you want them to make good decisions, then you need to think about giving their emotional brains what they need.

The good news is our irrational nature is somewhat predictable. Renowned behavioral psychologist Dan Ariely's best-selling book *Predictably Irrational*[3] can teach you everything you need to know about meeting people where they are emotionally. I worked with him at Intuit, and he has a lot of this figured out.

As voice and tone strategists we need to understand that we are doomed to fail with our voice and tone if we assume our customers are always thinking rationally. Decisions are emotional, not logical.[4] We need to meet people where they are, addressing their fear, shame, or irrational desires. Only after we succeed at that can we reach them where we need them to be—in their rational brains.

A strategic foundation for voice and tone

At this point, you should have what you need to build a strong foundation for your strategic approach. Figure 3.5 is an example of what the framework looks like once you have completed identifying customer needs and desires.

---

[4] See "Decisions are largely emotional, not logical"[9] by Jim Camp.

Building Block 1: Needs and Desires (but mostly desires)

Company vision:		
Become the most engaging consumer software solution in the world		
Goal for voice and tone:		
Go beyond the transactional to create a human-like relationship		
Customer needs:	**Customer desires:**	**Your character's desires:**
1. I need you to speak my language 2. I need you to guide me through each task 3. I need you to demystify complex things 4. I need to maintain control 5. I need you to help me get unstuck	1. I want you to treat me like a smart adult 2. I want to feel supported by you 3. I want to define what success feels like for me 4. I want you to turn my fear into ambition 5. I want you to recognize my sense of purpose in life	1. I want to help our customers succeed 2. I want to inspire the customer to feel confident 3. I want to be their go-to source for information 4. I want to create a safe place for the exchange of info 5. I want to turn their negative feelings into positive ones

Figure 3.5 – Strategic framework including customer needs and desires

In the next chapter, I look at how to create a set of principles that define your character in a way that can meet desires.

CHAPTER 4
Building Block 2: Defining an Archetype and Attributes

Writers are often coached to "find the voice of your characters." The same is true for the characters you create for your products and services. You must find their voice. But it's not as simple as you might think. Just as a novelist or screen writer spends time developing distinct characters, you must take the time to understand who your characters are before defining how they talk.

There's lots to learn about this. Aarron Walter's groundbreaking book *Designing for Emotion*[31], helps design teams answer the question, "If your product were a person, who would it be?" I take this a step further: how does that person *speak*.

Character attributes form the strategic foundation for your voice and tone strategy. However, I've worked with some teams who skipped over this step and went straight to building block 3—developing principles for their voice. Later, they backed their way into a set of character attributes (for example, "optimistic" could become an attribute for a principle like "talk about opportunities"). This can be a good way to break out of a stalemate, but I strongly recommend that you create a character definition and a set of voice attributes first.

Focus on the voice of your character

Your company may have created a character and a set of attributes as part of its brand strategy. If so, that may be enough to define your character's voice, and you can move on to developing voice principles. But in most cases, even with solid brand attributes in place, it's better to develop a separate character description with a subset of attributes just for voice. When Julie Newcome, a content strategist at Ultimate Software, was working with her product content team to define the character for their voice, they decided to do their own thing, separate from the brand marketing team.

"Marketing is a partner, but we don't need complete parity," she says. "We have to make sure we're doing what we need to do [with our product voice]. Our character is about how we speak to our customers in the product experience."[1]

So, consider developing a new character, one that's just for your voice, even if your marketing team has already created a well-defined character for your overall brand. It should have its own attributes, they should exist in concert with your brand character, without disrupting it.

Ask yourself, how would I describe our character—whether brand character or otherwise—based on a relationship established through voice. I could be something like, "when he talks he sounds like a coach." Then think about some adjectives you would use to describe that voice, such as "his voice is motivating." This is what you're after.

Use a modern archetype to identify your character

When defining a character as part of a voice and tone strategy—perhaps to complement an existing brand strategy—you need an identity for that character, one that connects with the specific needs of your customers (as exemplified by Newcome at Ultimate Software) before you do the harder work of figuring out how to describe its voice.

This is where archetypes can be powerful tools. An archetype is a character that plays a specific role in a story, such as the hero, villain, or mentor. For decades, marketing teams have used classic Jungian archetypes[2] like "the Ruler" or "the Sage." Instead, I recommend finding a more tangible archetype, pulled from everyday life, to connect with your customers and their needs. I've seen many content strategy teams brainstorm characters and land on descriptions like "helpful uncle" or "passionate teacher." These are good. They are modern in a way, but like the Jungian archetypes, they are

---
[1] Personal communication with the author.

[2] See Darbinyan Perch's article, "12 Brand Archetypes Revealed!"[27], for an introduction to Jungian Archetypes from a branding perspective.

still somewhat abstract. They have the power to connect, while still being universally understood.

Celebrities like Tom Hanks or Oprah Winfrey come up too, but because everyone has their own perceptions of real people, using one can derail your efforts. Once you go with an actual person, individuals will apply their own opinions, emotions, and experience. "Tom Hanks is too nice," someone will say. Or, "he's too bland." You'll never get past that.

It can be productive to start with someone like Tom Hanks, culled from a list of celebrities and other well-known people. But I recommend using that as a stepping stone to a more abstract, universally understood archetype. Ask yourselves, who does Tom Hanks embody? Is he a "trusted friend"? Now, that's an archetype everyone can get behind. Figure 4.1 has some examples of more modern archetypes.

- The copilot
- The tech-savvy friend
- The player's coach
- The clever sidekick
- The tour guide

Figure 4.1 – Modern archetypes that can work for voice

Using an adjective as part of the archetype name, for example the clever sidekick, can be effective. If you can identify an adjective that describes the character's overall purpose, try elevating it to the name. Proactive champion says, "this character's purpose is to figure out stuff and come to customers with options to help them succeed." Tech-savvy friend says, "this character is all about being a tech guru in the lives of the people they know."

Some teams take inspiration from their company's culture to get to the right archetype. "We have an amazing culture," Newcome says. "We decided we needed to exemplify that in our voice and tone. We needed to include that in our character."

Her team took the famous-person approach when they brainstormed possible characters. "We asked, 'if we were a person, what famous person would we be?' We put all these names on the wall. We said, 'you need to feel something about the person.'"

They took those descriptions of feelings about famous people, based on their customer needs and desires, and landed on an archetype with an adjective in the name, supported by a brief description (she asked that I not share it because it was still evolving).

Indeed, before working on the all-important set of voice attributes, you can help your strategic efforts by including a brief description with your character's name. Remember, you're focused on voice at this point, and that should come through in your description. Keep it brief.

> **The tech-savvy friend:** We are our customers' trusted source for info and advice on all things tech. We help them understand how to use tech and take pride in their accomplishments. But we also talk about opportunities. And we present new and exciting ways to conquer the fast-changing world of technology.

Create a set of voice attributes

At this point, you are ready to develop a set of attributes that describe how your character sounds when it talks. Of course, this is based on the set of customer needs and desires you developed for building block 1. You now need to ask yourself, who do we need to become to meet those desires?

Don't get too hung up on perfection at this point. You could spend days, weeks, or even months developing the perfect character. That shouldn't be your goal in the early stages of strategy development. Your goal should be to get something down on paper, something you're reasonably confident can lead you to a set of principles for voice, which is the topic of the next chapter. Once you experiment with a set of principles, you can always revisit your attributes to make them even better.

Brainstorm some attributes with your teams

If you haven't already, engage a cross-functional group of people from your organization in a brainstorming session around character. It's best if this group includes people from the various teams who are responsible for bringing your brand to life through voice and tone.

"Your brand is not only connected to your product and your marketing campaign," says Deborah Bosley, owner of Plain Language Group, which helps companies turn jargon into engaging conversations. "Your brand is connected to your terms and conditions; your brand is connected to the emails you send; your brand is connected to the chats you get into with customers." And that's why it's important to include a good cross section of content creators in the brainstorm.

It's also important to include a few key stakeholders, not just members of the design team. This way they will have some agency in the ultimate strategy. Buy in for any new approach comes quickest from those who helped define that approach. Also, engaging people from every function and group gives you the opportunity to help them see the value of voice.

Go broad then narrow

With your character archetype and a brief description as the target, go broad then narrow on a set of attributes for the voice of that character, maybe again employing the 2x2 method for narrowing ideas. Your goal is to identify three to five distinct adjectives that describe your archetype's voice. Any more than that and you risk watering down your character to the point where it is no longer distinctive.

Make lists of attributes. Put them down on paper, stickies, or a whiteboard. Then start to narrow. You can do this by putting your list of customer needs and desires next to your list of attributes. As a team, ask yourselves, which of these attributes best meet those needs and desires? Circle individual needs and desires and then circle corresponding attributes. If your customer wants to become an expert, then a corresponding attribute you embody could be something like "knowledgeable" or "wise."

When narrowing, consider attributes that lead your character to take on a more distinctive personality. For example, "clever" is more distinctive than "smart." It speaks to someone who uses their smartness in a quick or sharp way—someone who might even be described as ingenious. For that reason, "clever" can bring a more human-like personality. But be sure you're not just trying to turn something like "smart" into something more by using an adjective like "clever." Think about your goal. Does it align with it?

Narrow to a list of three to five. If you're brainstorming in groups, consider a separate session for you and a smaller core team to pull multiple sets of attributes into one. You want to move forward with a tight set of adjectives that supports your character description, something like, "We are a tech-savvy friend, and when we speak, we become knowledgeable, perceptive, and sharp."

Put guardrails around your attributes

Once you have a working set of attributes, consider putting a qualifying guardrail on each one to help your team understand what you mean and where your voice falls on a spectrum. One successful and widely used approach is "this, not that." If one of your attributes is perceptive, you could make that clearer and more useful by saying, "perceptive, but not nosey." Adding the simple guardrail "not nosey" helps writers focus. More importantly, it can help you craft focused principles.

Putting guardrails on attributes is more effective for voice and tone than another commonly used approach, which is to extend the attribute with some context. In that method, if you are passionate, you might say that you are "passionate in nature." That works well for overall brand characteristics, but it's less specific and, therefore, less useful for writers.

Once you have your attributes, complete with qualifying guardrails, consider a brief description or a set of bullet points for each attribute to further clarify what you mean. For example: "We are… Perceptive, but not nosey."

We use what we know about you to not only answer your immediate question, but also to give you exactly what you need to move forward without you having to ask for it. We understand the intent behind what you're saying, regardless of how you're saying it.

Figure 4.2 shows the attributes Shopify declared in their voice and tone strategy. They used guardrails for each attribute, followed by three succinct bullets to make it clear what they mean.

Voice guidelines

Shopify is always:

CONFIDENT, NOT ARROGANT

- Use expertise to help merchants succeed, don't talk down to them
- Be plain-spoken, not pretentious
- Be specific when explaining a merchant benefit without making a feature sound better than it is

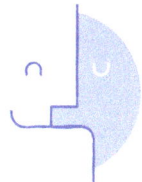

EMPATHETIC, NOT OVERPROTECTIVE

- Communicate in a way that respects merchant emotions and situations
- Offer merchants encouragement and practical advice
- Clearly explain how merchants will be impacted when something goes wrong, but don't over-explain with redundant content

TRANSPARENT, NOT BLUNT

- Be upfront and honest with merchants, even if we make a mistake
- Back up claims with facts and data
- Communicate with clarity and empathy—be direct, not insensitive

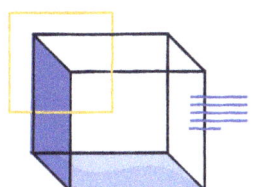

Figure 4.2 – Shopify character attributes[3]

---

[3] Shopify voice and tone guidelines [https://polaris.shopify.com/content/-voice-and-tone#section-voice-guidelines]

Consider tone

Once you've defined some attributes (don't get too hung up on perfection at this point. It's best to move forward and circle back later if you need to), you might be asking about tone. If these attributes describe who you are when you talk, doesn't that include tone?

The simple answer is yes, but it's not that simple. Remember, tone flexes to situations in context. Voice attributes are about who you are as a character, the relationship you create. Tone is about how you tap into the mood of the moment, the emotion created by a specific situation. It's a powerful part of how we talk.

"Feeling good is really important," says Bosley of Plain Language Group. "If I just get my frustration alleviated I am delighted. It doesn't take a lot to make people feel good. We want to feel like the problem is solved. I don't need to feel loved, just taken care of. Tone can address that."

Consider "perceptive" as an attribute. It doesn't speak to tone, but tone is governed by it. You might be broadly perceptive in how you speak to your customer's needs, but how you use tone to express that attribute depends on the situation. If the customer is making progress and likely feeling positive about it, perceptive might sound something like:

> "Hey there. Now that we've set up access to your child's grades, let's consider looking at using your smartphone to easily track their school schedule."

You're perceiving the need to do something more and then talking about it as an opportunity. In a situation where you expect the customer to have less-than-positive feelings, perceptive could sound something like:

> "Your child's grades are all in one place. If you also want to track their schedules, it's not as simple. But there are good options."

You still perceive the need, but you are flexing to the situation with a more direct, helpful tone, while still sounding positive. Shopify also has some useful guidelines for this, using a "this, not that" framework, as shown in Figure 4.3, which shows guidelines for a positive situation and Figure 4.4, which shows guidelines for a negative situation.[4]

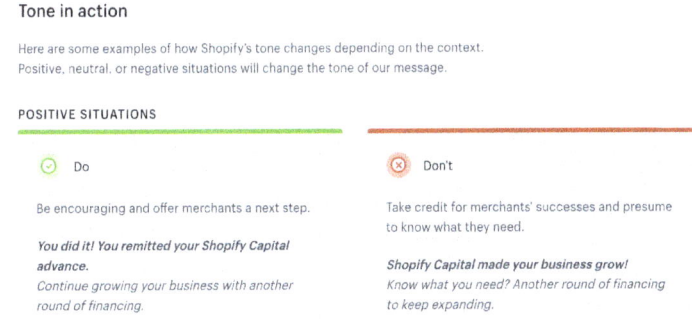

Figure 4.3 – Shopify guidelines for positive situations

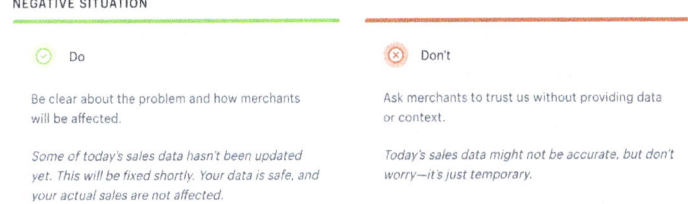

Figure 4.4 – Shopify guidelines for negative situations

These two examples show the difference between voice and tone. Voice is about character, tone is about situations. Voice is identified with a set of attributes, tone with a set of guidelines. I'll talk more about how to treat each of these when I cover flex frameworks in Chapter 6.

Test your attributes before moving forward

After Newcome and her team at Ultimate Software came up with an archetype and some attributes, they decided to test what they had before moving

---

[4] Both of these examples are from the Shopify voice and tone guidelines [https://polaris.shopify.com/content/voice-and-tone#section-voice-guidelines]

into principles and guidelines. This is good design practice. Just as it's important to validate customer needs and desires using secondary testing, it's a good idea to test your attributes. You can use scrappy, guerrilla testing methods—ambushing people in coffee shops, etc.—or a more formal research method, as Newcome's team did.

"We did a focus group," Newcome says. "We found out that there isn't just one archetype that describes us, there are several, from which we drew a number of attributes. We decided we needed to build our own archetype. Then we decided to make posters of it and put them up in our offices. That way we all understand the voice and tone in the context of the archetype. The voice and tone need to support who we are."

OK, you have a goal for your voice and tone, you've narrowed to some strategic customer needs and desires, and you've landed on an archetype description for your character. You've also done the hard work of coming up with three to five attributes that describe your character's voice. Some might say that's enough, "Let's start writing content. We know who we are. We know who the customer is. Let's get busy engaging in their story and connecting with them!"

Hold up. Without a guiding set of principles, you can't craft game-changing content. You still need to know how you are going to bring your character's voice to life. You can declare that you're perceptive, but how are you going to use that attribute in practice? That's what I cover next, the most strategic and useful part of any voice and tone strategy: Principles.

CHAPTER 5
Building Block 3: Crafting Principles to Guide Your Voice

The most useful part of your voice and tone strategy is the set of principles you craft to define and guide your team. Attributes define who you are. Principles bring those attributes to life through voice.

In its purest form a principle is a rule for implementing a proposed system of belief or behavior. Put simply, it dictates how you should act and why. For product designers, this involves how you act on your customer's needs and help them succeed in using your products and services. And for content designers, it's about how you use words and voice.

When crafting a new set of principles, you'll be faced with hard choices. You need to pick a direction for each and run with it. You also need to be willing to let go of some things that may be working well in order to make space for an even more strategic approach. When I worked with the Quickbooks team at Intuit to help them develop a set of principles for voice,[1] we ended up with a mix of both legacy principles, such as "Keep it simple," and new, more aspirational ones like "It's about them, not us."

Know the difference between a principle and an attribute

Many teams confuse or even blur the lines between attributes and principles. Both speak to customer needs and desires. Each can operate independently. But they play distinct roles. So, I usually start discussions about principles by getting alignment on how and why they are different from attributes.

"Optimistic" is an attribute. "Bring optimism into the conversation" is a principle. The attribute defines a characteristic. The principle describes how a character might become optimistic. "Authentic, but not gratuitous"

---
[1] Vince Teodoro, "Intuit Quickbooks Voice and Tone Principles"[30].

is an attribute with a guardrail, and "Celebrate their successes" is a principle that could bring authenticity to life in a specific way.

I once led and coached a design team for the financial management app Mint that developed and updated Mint's strategy for voice and tone. At the start we were presented with an existing strategy that blurred the lines between attributes and principles. In fact, principles and attributes were in one mixed bag:

When speaking to customers, the Mint character will:

- Be optimistic, but realistic
- Be smart, but down to Earth
- Keep it simple, but magical

Using the verb "being" to describe "optimistic" and "smart" identifies them as attributes the Mint character embodied, but the verb "keeping" in "keeping things simple" blurs the line between the attribute of being simple and the principle of using simplicity to bring the character to life in a specific way. After much research, brainstorming, and discussion, we kept optimistic, smart, and magical as attributes, complete with guardrails, and then crafted a set of principles to guide the writers and content designers. Here is the result:

Mint is…

- Optimistic, but realistic
- Smart, but down to Earth
- Magical, but functional

When Mint speaks, we…

- Talk about possibilities
- Treat the customer like a responsible adult
- Use data to make meaningful connections

Principles don't need to track one-to-one with attributes. There's always going to be some overlap. And some principles will speak to more than one attribute. However, if you start by drawing a line from each principle to an attribute, it can help the team get on the right track and feel confident about where they're headed. For example, optimistic → Talk about opportunities.

Another thing worth considering is the difference between a design principle and a voice principle. Think about the customer problems you're design team is trying to solve. How will you tackle them? Once you've grounded yourself and your team in the nature and purpose of the higher-level design principles behind your product or service, you'll be ready to develop principles that guide the creation of voice and tone within your overall design.

Craft principles with writers in mind

Your principles for voice show writers how to speak to your customers through content. Therefore, they must make sense to writers. Voice principles should not only illustrate the relationship between your character and your customers, they should speak to the craft of writing, just as principles for visual design or motion design should speak to the designers crafting those parts of the experience.

On the Mint team, we had "Keep it simple" as a guiding principle for voice. It's good as a broader design principle, too. But what does it really mean for voice, and how does a writer follow that principle? It's open to a lot of interpretation.

A good voice principle minimizes the need for interpretation. It's clear and specific about what to do. And it's focused on the action of speaking. "Keep it simple" would be a lot more useful to writers if it spoke to a specific way to make things simple with content, for example, "Use common language for complex things," or "Speak to what's needed and leave out the rest."

Obviously, any specificity you give to a principle stems from your voice attributes and your customer needs and desires. At the most basic level, your customer might need you to "Speak my language." Your character's voice might connect to that by becoming "approachable." And one of your principles for how to speak to that could be "Open doors with simple conversations."

Think about the verbs you put into the titles of your principles, for example: "talk," "speak," or "Let them know…." Are they actions a writer or content designer would take when creating voice? Back that up with a short description for each principle. Here is an example:

> **Talk about data as a connection to people like them**
> When appropriate, shed light on the meaningful connections that access to information can make with people, places, and things. While our technology enables the use of data to do magical things, our voice is how we can make it relevant to our customers.

Make sure your principles are strategic

Writing a strategic principle requires an understanding of what makes it strategic, rather than a tactic you would employ in service to your strategy. Principles guide us in why we're saying what we're saying and how we can achieve our goal through voice. Tactics are the coherent actions we might take along the way when employing that strategy. The line between the two can seem blurry, and that's OK. What's important is that you craft a set of principles that is more than just a set of tactical actions. Otherwise, your strategy could fail.

In his thought provoking article, "The difference between strategy and tactics"[26], Jeremiah Owyang says, "we use the terms strategy and tactics interchangeably and in a haphazard manner. When probing at online definitions and dictionaries, the two often share many of the same characteristics, making them difficult to differentiate."

It's important that you understand the difference. If all you're doing is defining tactics without first crafting principles that speak to the higher goal, you're not really being strategic. It is easy to write principles that should really be guidelines.

Consider these two potential principles: "Use short, action-oriented sentences" and "Talk about opportunities." The first is tactical and, therefore, more of a guideline than a principle. It guides you to do something tangible and doesn't connect with your customer's desires. On the other hand, "Talk about opportunities" is strategic. This principle speaks to who you are as a character, connects to a customer desire to get better at something, and supports a goal of engaging customers to become advocates for your product. That makes it strategic.

Ultimately, your strategic principles work in tandem with a set of tactical guidelines that you'll define later. A tactic you could use to "talk about opportunities" might be "create a series of notifications that tie current successes to future opportunities." A tangible tactic like this is tied to a specific priority and identifies actions you will take for a particular project.

Although tactics aren't part of the strategic building blocks, they are a big part of the guidelines for structure and style that you'll create when it comes time to implement your strategy. With principles as a guide, you can define tactical ways to deliver your content with specific rules for style and structure. I'll talk more about that in Chapter 8.

As a strategist, you'll sometimes find yourself working in businesses that love to jump to tactics. They need to get stuff done, so they pursue lists of priorities and skip the strategy. That approach often leads to failure.[2]

Go for the aspirational

We all have aspirations (most of us, anyway), and we love to talk about them. "If I win the lottery, I'm going to buy everyone I love their own big house," is a common refrain in our dream-centric culture. Think about your own aspirations. They're probably about something big, and they're likely defined by strong emotion. And that, just as with desires, is what makes them a strategic opportunity.

---

[2] For an entertaining look at how content strategists can help avoid this situation, see Melissa Ward's blog post, which talks about a conference presentation by Kristina Halvorson, "Don't Stand There With Your Mouth Open"[32].

Indeed, going for aspirational things is about going after desire. Principles help you appeal to aspirations in a strategic way, which means talking about something more than everyday needs.

But that often creates a conflict. As content designers, we still need to help people through transactional activities. That's why so many voice principles are about basic things such as "be conversational," or "demystify the complex." They are important, but they're what I like to call "no-duh" principles. You need to have them, but you should also put some aspirational principles in the mix. If you who have reached a point where principles like "be conversational" or "lead the way" cause you and your team to say, "no duh," you may want to consider setting them aside temporarily, so you can craft a list of principles that speak to higher things.

> What is an aspirational principle?
> Start by asking yourself:
>
> - Does it speak to emotion?
> - Does it focus on helping people improve, understand, or overcome something?
> - Does it speak to achievement or success?
> - Does it elevate the conversation and bring maturity to the relationship?

"Be conversational" focuses on how to speak to customers in a way that connects to what they need. Compare that to a principle like "Speak to their higher self." This principle connects to a desire to feel smart, be strong, and to conquer whatever difficulties stand in their way. It guides your character to elevate the conversation from one that is focused on actions to one that speaks to bigger things. As such, it has the potential to increase the level of engagement you have with your customers.

Aspirational principles can also focus on overcoming negative emotions or avoiding them all together. "Turn self-doubt into determination" is a good example of an aspirational principle that speaks to a customer's desire to overcome fear.

Building Block 3: Crafting Principles to Guide Your Voice

At TurboTax, my product and marketing content team recognized that the story our customers were telling themselves about using our product was, "it's going to be difficult and scary, and I'm probably going to suck at it." Up until that point, our voice and tone principles emphasized ease of use. We convinced a lot of people to try us out. But we didn't recognize that in doing so we were making customers vulnerable to feelings of failure and incompetence.

Suppose someone tells you over and over that some task is easy. Then you reach a point in the experience where it seems very difficult. If you're already feeling vulnerable, you might start telling yourself, "this is supposed to be easy, but it's not. Is it just me?" Shame sets in. A little voice inside your head might say, "I should be good at this, but I'm not." And you'd probably run for the door. Many of our customers did just that.

So, as part of bringing our new character to life, the TurboTax team crafted a new principle for our voice: "Understand their vulnerability." This led to big changes in the way we talked to customers.

The voice of our character went from "TurboTax is as easy as 1, 2, 3" to "Taxes are complex. But we'll be by your side to conquer them together."

We reinforced this throughout the experience, and it connected. Our customers voluntarily told us that we understood them. Our conversion numbers went up, as did our retention rates.

The same approach works for those of you crafting enterprise content for human resources or employee engagement. Understand the story your employees tell themselves, define a voice that can connect with that story, and then help them reach for the stars by following principles that consider their emotions while speaking to their aspirations. Figure 5.1 shows some examples of no-duh and aspirational principles.

Principles fall into two categories:

No-duh (We always will…)	Aspirational (We strive to…)
Be conversational	Talk about opportunities
Lead the way	Speak to their higher self
Maintain accuracy	Let them know we're listening
Use plain English	Turn self-doubts into determination
Demystify the complex	Use data to make meaningful connections

Figure 5.1 – No-duh versus aspirational principles

One good way to distinguish no-duh principles from aspirational principles is to use below-the-neck verbs versus above-the-neck verbs. Below-the-neck verbs are simple actions, such as: "continue," "enter," "put," or "tell." Above-the-neck verbs encourage higher thinking: "plan," "consider," "think about," or "recognize." Aspirational principles will lead you to use more above-the-neck verbs. And that can elevate the relationship to one that's perceived as more mature and meaningful.

Treat your principles like an open toolbox

As you find the right voice through the trial and error of rolling out an initial version of your strategy, don't be afraid to update or add to your principles along the way. While writing content for a new product line at a travel services company in San Francisco, I was asked to craft a totally new voice for properties that appeal to high-end clients. The team needed to do this in line with a brand-new strategy for cutting-edge and, some might say, sassy content.

The marketing team thought they knew what the customer wanted, and they created a strategy that seemed right. But once the writers started writing, it became clear that the principles needed an update. The attributes, for the most part, were still right. But as we wrote content and figured out how to really bring it to life in a way that differentiated us from competitors, the principles changed. We realized they were too tactical in nature. They weren't strategic enough.

The initial list included mostly tactical principles such as the following:

> **Punch it up**
> Use short, impactful sentences to show a little bit of attitude or tongue-in-cheek sass.

We updated it to include more strategic principles, such as the following:

> **Balance talk of relaxation with a desire to party**
> Not everything or everyone at our properties is about loafing in a pool or enjoying the view from a lounge chair. You can fix a drink to be enjoyed poolside, or you can hold court at the bar.

It wasn't until we actually started writing and delivering content that we recognized the need to tweak the principles to optimize our strategy.

Tactics can still infiltrate this process, so beware. Based on what I was asked to do, I considered adding a principle that stated, "Use metaphors and analogies to tell a story." But that is a tactic. A principle needs to stay focused on the behavior, so we came up with "Tell a story about the experience they will have." Using metaphors and analogies was a tactic we could use to do that.

Create a subset of principles for specific projects and priorities

Once you have an over-all set of principles for your voice, you may find certain projects call for a bit more definition. Projects and priorities come and go. They are tactical, and they often provide the most realistic application of your strategy for voice and tone.

Building Block 3: Crafting Principles to Guide Your Voice

You may be working on a project or priority and discover that although the overall voice and tone principles are great, they don't address the specific needs of the customer in this touchpoint or speak to the problem you're trying to solve with this feature. In that case, consider creating a subset of two to three principles just for your project.

Let's say your overall principles are the following:

- Put them in charge
- Talk about opportunities
- Help them understand
- Let them know we're always with them

These are solid principles for how you might speak to customers across a broad set of experiences. They empower the customer, they are relationship building, and they include some aspirational thinking.

Now let's say you're working on a project that uses new technology to deliver personalized answers to questions about their situation. This new feature is supported nicely by your principle of "help them understand," but your customer is bit further down in the weeds. Your objective might be to build their confidence in accomplishing a particular task at a point where they're stuck and need you to help them move forward.

In that case, you might consider a project-specific set of voice principles to help writers deliver against those specific needs. This set could look something like the following:

- Let them know they're still in control
- Don't leave them hanging
- Help them accept the outcome

These principles are more specific to customers using your new feature, but they're not tactics. They complement, but don't override, your overall principles.

Talking about these kinds of complementary principles, which meet customer needs in a particular feature or touchpoint within a broader experience, is the perfect transition to the next chapter: flexing your voice and tone. This is where I talk about the strategic opportunities that flex frameworks offer to your writers, content strategists, and brand marketers.

CHAPTER 6
Flex Voice and Tone

Just as your personality and mood vary depending on the situation, your voice and tone must flex to match the different situations your customers might find themselves in. Let's look at a framework for flexing your voice and tone at the right time and in the right way.

A flex framework, one that utilizes your character attributes and voice principles, can help you and your writing teams address customer needs at different touchpoints. For example, a sign-in procedure and the medical questionnaire that follows may be part of the same service, but the customer experience varies as customers go from sign-in to the questionnaire.

How do voice and tone flex?

Voice flexes depending on the situation

Imagine you're at work. You're in a meeting with your team or a few senior leaders, presenting content you've worked hard on for a couple of weeks. How would you sound?

Professional? Composed? To the point?

Probably. You might even follow a set of principles that include such guidance as "stay focused on the topic" or "keep humor to a minimum."

Now imagine you're with that same group at a happy-hour event after work. You're laughing and letting loose after a long day or week, benefiting from some camaraderie in a shared experience that's more about social bonds than professional goals.

How would you sound then? You probably wouldn't be thinking about principles for how you're talking, but if you did, they might be things like "find common ground," "use humor to break the ice," or "talk about family and friends."

I once bumped into my doctor, Steve, at a festival. We struck up a conversation and had a laugh as we walked around, snacking on corn dogs. During the time we chatted, his voice was quite different from our conversations in his examination room, where he is reserved, concerned, and inquisitive. At the festival he still seemed like Steve, but he flexed his voice, becoming more irreverent and cheeky during our festival interaction.

Tone flexes depending on emotion

In the doctor's office, Dr. Steve flexed his tone, too. Once he had to tell me something sounded strange in my lungs and that he was ordering an MRI. He momentarily took on a more comforting tone to address my concern. Then he shifted back. Tone flexes to the emotion of the moment; voice flexes to the situation or touchpoint.

At work, if you are interacting with an employee who has just experienced a death in the family, your tone will be empathetic and reassuring. If you are interacting with an employee who has just completed a successful project, your tone will be enthusiastic and congratulatory.

Build a voice flex framework

I will begin with a framework for flexing voice. The list of needs and desires you created in building block 1 is the starting place. This list gives you a start, but you need to flex to more specific needs and desires that arise as customers use different parts of your product or service.

At TurboTax, we originally took the position that our character's voice would be consistent across products, features, and experiences and that only tone would flex. Our strategy included a character based on a hero and a mentor, some aspirational principles, and some examples. The writers were ready to go, but once they started writing, things got tough.

This was especially true for the marketing team writing content for Turbo-Tax.com website. They understood how brand attributes, such as trustworthy and ingenious, worked for our product copy, but those attributes didn't meet the needs of our customers during the sales process, when they were deciding whether to use the product. We needed guidance on how to connect with people at that point.

Our new strategy focused on empowering customers to take control of their taxes and their money. Although our empowerment principles worked for the product content on our website, something was missing: we needed to flex our voice to be persuasive.

I pulled together a cross-functional team from marketing, product, customer care, and social media/PR. We mapped out the end-to-end customer journey, focusing on identifying customers' needs and desires as they moved from one touchpoint to the next. After a lot of iteration and feedback from other team members across groups, we built a framework that shows customer needs at each touchpoint (see Figure 6.1).

Figure 6.1 – Map of customer end-to-end journey

Identify flexes for your touchpoints

Once you've mapped out customer needs for each touchpoint, the next step is to develop flexes to meet each need. From building block 2, you have a set of voice attributes for your character. Do these attributes cover everything you need at each individual touchpoint or are there gaps, such as the need to sound persuasive when the customer is in your marketing space or reassuring when the customer is looking for help?

If so, add those attributes to your existing list. Brainstorm possible attributes to fill any gaps. Then narrow them to a short list. The goal is to compile a list of attributes that writers can use as flexes at each the touchpoints.

In addition to creating a list of flexes, you also need to determine how those flexes overlap. Just as with your company's high-level list of brand attributes, your voice flexes come together in different ways to meet the needs of your customers. At one point you might flex to be both empowering and inspiring and at another only empowering.

Incorporating this overlap means you need a framework that allows for more than one flex attribute to be assigned to each touchpoint. To do this, I recommend the following steps:

1. Make a list of flexes that can cover all your touchpoints
2. Identify the touchpoints that each flex will be used in
3. Assign the different customer needs each flex can address in each touchpoint
4. Consider a subset of voice attributes for each flex that help your writers bring it to life

At TurboTax, we created a map for each flex that described:

- Where customers are in the experience (the touchpoint)
- What they are trying to do (tasks or decisions within a touchpoint)
- What their needs are as they do those things (including emotional desires)
- What subset of voice attributes can we could use to meet those needs (three sub attributes for each flex)

This framework showed the flex attribute followed by the touchpoint it was assigned to. The touchpoints drove the creation of the flexes, but I prefer to organize the framework based on the high-level flex attributes, which for TurboTax included: persuasive, empowering, and dedicated. Figure 6.2 shows our flex framework.

Flex Voice and Tone 63

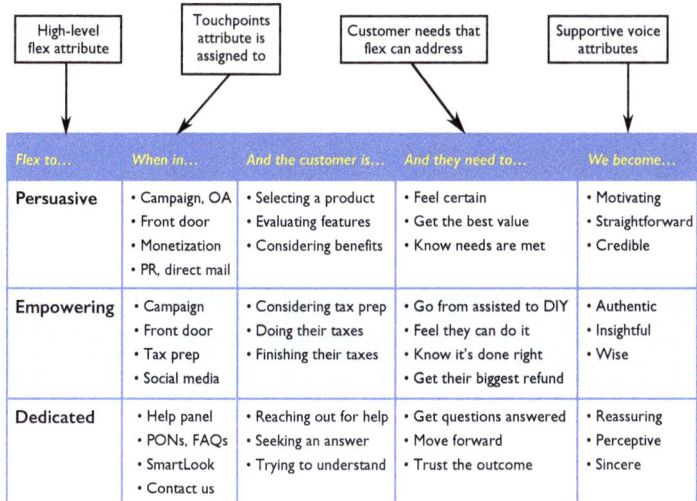

Figure 6.2 – TurboTax voice flex framework

This model gives you high-level flex attributes—persuasive, empowering, and dedicated—along with more specific, supportive voice attributes that target customer needs and desires at particular touchpoints. This framework doesn't discard the attributes you created in building block 2. It incorporates them into the flex framework by designating them as either high-level flex attributes or specific voice attributes that support one of those flexes.

Figure 6.3 – TurboTax voice flex end-to-end flexes

In addition to this, you can create a supporting graphic that illustrates the overlap of flexes to give your writers even more direction. Figure 6.3 uses the end-to-end model from Figure 6.2 and shows which flex or combination of flexes you need for each touchpoint.

Create principles for your voice flex framework

You might find it helpful to develop the framework further by creating principles for the flex attributes you just created. Suppose you created the following principles in building block 3:

- Talk about opportunities
- Speak their language
- Help them understand

These are great for helping writers bringing your character's voice to life. However, they may not fit some of your touchpoints. For example, if you have "persuasive" as a flex attribute for your website landing pages, you could create principles for how to sound persuasive.

Figure 6.4 shows how you might create subsets of principles that support a particular overall voice principle.

Overall voice principles		
Talk about opportunities Speak their language Help them understand		
Flex voice principles		
Persuasive	Empowering	Dedicated
■ Dramatize the benefit ■ Substantiate the value ■ Show, don't tell	■ Put them in charge ■ Use encouraging language ■ Talk about the future	■ Meet their need instantly ■ Don't be ambiguous ■ Give them closure

Figure 6.4 – Flex voice principles

Flexing tone

Whether you have a smaller product, where momentary tone flexes are enough, or a larger product, where broader voice changes are helpful, a framework for flexing tone is a powerful tool that can help you get it right.

Flexing tone is a delicate thing. One word in a sentence can create a very different mood. Consider the word "please" in this question: "Jeff, can you update your personal info before we continue?" vs. "Jeff, can you please update your info before we continue?"

Does the word "please" sound polite? Or is it demanding? There's nuance in how this word is used. And the context can influence how readers perceive a word. The word "sorry" is another good example. You might think it's always good to apologize when things go wrong. But you are speaking through a user interface, and an apology may not be perceived as authentic and friendly. Customers may actually perceive an apology as phony and think that you are indifferent to their needs or even manipulative.

Ask yourself:

- How will my customers feel about what I'm saying based on the context?
- What are the different ways this could be perceived?

To address the need for momentary flexes in tone, you can create a map similar to the voice flex map, create guidelines, or do both.

Look at mapping tone end-to-end

Suppose you have a principle around being friendly and sounding lighthearted, or even fun. Bobbie Wood, a founder of the online writing program UXWritersCollective, who has worked as a content strategist for both Google and Intuit, points out that although this principle can work well in many situations, if your customer is having a tough time and sees an error message, your voice shouldn't sound fun. It should sound like you take the issue seriously and want to solve the problem. That's why it's helpful to think of tone as a set of sliding controls that can be turned up or down as needed.

You can adjust the tone based on the audience, the situation, and the primary goal or task of your customer at that moment. The choice of words and messaging sets the tone, which in turn influences how customers feel about what's happening.

To help her teams and her students succeed at this, Wood created an end-to-end map that flexes tone on a scale from fun to serious. She then identified key instances along a possible customer journey in which tone could flex (see Figure 6.5).

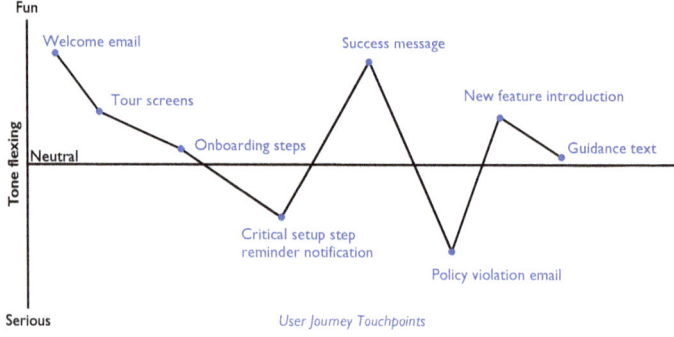

Figure 6.5 – Flexing tone across the customer journey[1]

The y-axis in Figure 6.5 shows a scale that ranges from fun to serious. In a success message, for example, the tone would be more fun, maybe sounding lighthearted and celebratory. The x-axis shows customer touchpoints.

Your product or service might call for different end points on the y-axis. For example, if you're creating content for a site that supports mental health, the two end points could be "warm" and "warning." Messages of support for someone who's not feeling well should sound warm, but you may also need warnings against unhealthy behaviors.[2]

---

[1] Graphic used with permission from Bobbie Wood.

[2] To learn more about this, check out "The Four Dimensions of Tone of Voice"[23] and "Tone-of-Voice Words"[24] by Kate Moran of the Nielsen Norman Group.

Create guidelines for tone flexes

Take "playfulness" as a possible tone flex. When used well, playfulness can deepen your relationship with customers and create stronger connections, but it's not something you should sustain across the experience. It comes with the risk of eroding confidence. That's why it's not a principle for voice, but rather a flex in tone, one you can use at the right moment, given the right context. If you were using it in conjunction with the tone map in Figure 6.5, it might come into play in the welcome and the success message.

I recommend you create a set of guidelines for flexes like these. This can complement the tone map or replace it. Here's how to do that:

Start with a customer desire:

"I want you to turn my negative feelings about finances into positive ones."

Identify what they're feeling:

- Less than successful
- Incompetent
- Afraid of managing money
- Not keeping up with their peers
- A sense of shame: "I should know this stuff."

Make a list of possible tone flexes that can connect with those emotions:

- Playfulness
- Commiseration
- Sympathy
- Celebration
- Humor

Now create specific guidelines for each possible flex that includes opportunities and desired outcomes. Figure 6.6 shows guidelines for using the tone flex playfulness.

Tone flex: Playfulness
Playfulness can strip negative feelings away. By sounding playful, at just the right moment, you can open the door to more encouraging language. Think of negative feelings as a roadblock and playfulness as a plow that breaks through it. Being playful is not an end in itself. It's a means to an end: The emotional connection underlying it. Used when the timing is right, it opens up the door to even deeper levels of engagement and reduces defensiveness.

Opportunities for playfulness:	The desired customer response:
■ Celebration of completion and/or reward ■ Pointing out behaviors that make us human ■ Uncovering surprising opportunities ■ Relating to others who face the same challenges	■ "Wow. You get me." ■ "Hah! That's funny because it's true." ■ "I feel so much better since you pointed that out."

Figure 6.6 – Guidelines for the tone flex playfulness

Deciding whether to flex voice or tone

Your flex framework will vary based on your product, its size, and how much the needs of your customers vary. A focused product from a smaller company may just need a flex framework for tone. On the other hand, a large company with many products may need to flex both voice and tone.

"The world of Google is massive," Bobbie Wood said, "It's billions of customers. When I think about the voice changing, it's because the scale of the company is so huge. If I think about writing for TurboTax, I'm writing for customers with a similar task. They are dealing with taxes. Still, both Google and TurboTax try really hard to have a unified brand."

When Aarron Walter, author of *Designing for Emotion*[31], and Kate Kiefer Lee, co-author of *Nicely Said: Writing for the Web with Style and Purpose*[14], created a design persona for MailChimp, they wrote a clear set of principles for voice and guidelines for tone that could remain largely consistent across touchpoints, because the focus of their service was relatively narrow.

For TurboTax, taxes are the focus, but they are handled differently across a suite of products and services. This requires flexes in voice to meet varying customer needs. And Google presents a world of flexing opportunities across many products. Figure 6.7 shows some possible approaches to flexing for several different companies.

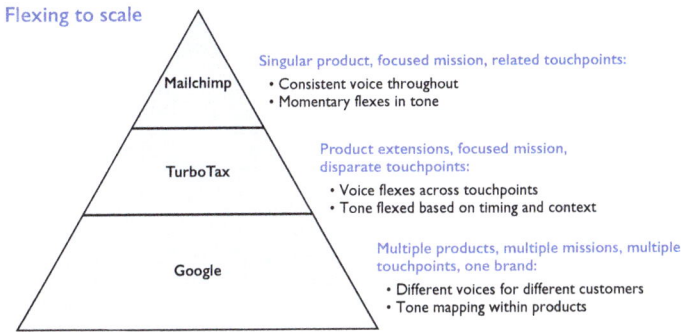

Figure 6.7 – Flex voice and tone based on the product or service

Flex frameworks and expanding products or services

The approaches outlined in this chapter also work well for adapting an existing voice and tone framework for a new product or service. Think about Amazon. They've got numerous product experiences under one brand umbrella, and they add new offerings frequently. Their design team likely wants a consistent brand character across all of their products and services. That means one big strategy, with flexes for different experiences.

Smaller companies may not want different voice and tone strategies for each product. If that's you, consider a flex framework for your *conversational user interface* (chatbot or voice user interface). Maintain your high-level character attributes while flexing, for example, to a customer using a chatbot or voice-based interface.

In a world full of contraptions that can understand human speech, UX writers and content designers must understand that relationships between humans and robots (physical or digital) must be built on something that seems authentic. That may require frameworks for flexing voice and tone.

That also includes voice and tone for regional product experiences. A customer in France will have very different expectations around language than one in the U.S. Flex frameworks can help with that.

Now that we've covered three of the main strategy building blocks for voice and tone, walked through some useful ways to use them as you flex to varying customer needs, it's time to put them into practice. In the next chapter, I'll cover the fourth and final voice and tone strategy building block: Examples.

CHAPTER 7
Building Block 4: The Power of Examples

Examples are the final building block in the Vertical Voice and Tone Strategy. In this step, you apply everything you've built—most importantly your principles—to some creative work. You'll want to carve out the necessary time to create the best examples possible.

It's a cliché, but it still rings true: A picture is worth a thousand words. You can go on and on describing your character in great detail, using colorful words for each attribute, but all those words won't have the same power to describe your voice as a carefully crafted example. That's why I recommend keeping the descriptions for attributes and principles to just two or three sentences. Lay out what they are, then let the examples do the talking. In my experience, that's the best way to get skeptical and confused listeners nodding and giving you comments like, "ah, now I get it."

"Good examples help to bring non-writers along," says Danielle D'Agostino, a content strategist who has worked on political campaigns and for software design teams at Instagram and Amazon. "Even showing examples of your product's current content helps. It can make the argument, 'if we don't unlock this new strategy, this is how bad the experience will continue to be.'"

Seniors leaders probably won't care about your attributes and principles, anyway, adds Michelle McAlister, a content strategist who has worked for the likes of Airbnb and LinkedIn. "They don't want to know about your strategy, they just want to be provoked," she says. "The strategy is the *how*, they care about the *what*. They don't understand principles, they just know what sounds good. They want to see the examples."

Start with "just-dos"

Once you have your strategy's initial building blocks defined—goal, customer desires, attributes, and principles—there may be a push by some on your content team to try them out on some of their current project work. Sometimes things are moving too fast to go through the process of putting together a durable set of voice and tone examples before getting into the actual work. In that case, you can ask writers to test the strategy by applying the principles to current work, what I call "just-dos."

Whether or not you have time to work on a more durable set of examples for your strategy, you can satisfy the urge for some just-dos by working with your team to make a list of things they can work on right away, usually related to current work. For example, a content designer working on microcopy for a set of push notifications or alerts could try out your new voice and tone principles without much risk, advancing your strategy in the process and possibly giving you content you can use for examples.

However, keep just-dos to a minimum until you've had a chance to communicate your new strategy to the leaders in your organization, including marketing strategists, product managers, design leads, and others. Just-dos are a good way for the content team to test your new approach, but they shouldn't be so disruptive that other leaders see it as an abrupt, untested change in direction.

Here are some examples of tasks that could be used as just-dos:

- A chat initiation model on a home page
- Account creation microcopy
- Simple, short security messages
- Subheads on a form
- An employee-focused alert on an internal site

Longer pieces, such as articles, landing page copy, success screens, and error messages, may be too much of a reach for a just-do, especially if your new strategy represents something bold and potentially provocative. It's fine to give your content creators some just-dos, but you also need to give them time to help you craft the examples you'll need to get buy-in from people who may see your strategy as unproven, experimental, or risky. A durable set of examples—whether drawn from current designs or mock ups of new concepts—can get the broader teams in your organization on board.

Create examples to inspire and instruct

In addition to showing writers what to do, examples should also clearly demonstrate the possibilities. Go for aspiration. Push the limits of your new voice and tone. You can always dial it back to the right level once you get a sense of what's possible. Creating examples gives you the opportunity to get out of your comfort zone and try something different.

Print out your new principles and put them up in your design space. Use a big font. If you've created a flex framework, print it out as well, along with any subsets of principles that are tied to flex attributes. Then print out some screenshots from your existing product experience or website and put them up next to the principles. Your initial set of existing screenshots can represent bigger projects and broader experiences than your just-dos, and they should provide an end-to-end view of your character's voice as it might build and grow across the experience.

Take time to consider how the principles will come to life as you talk to your customers and how your new character will sound. Invite project leaders and other non-designers to review the principles with you. This kind of collaboration will both generate ideas for your examples and build support for your new strategy.

Next, create some assignments for your writers. Ask them what they'd like to work on, but consider mixing things up. For example, you might encourage someone who usually works on marketing content to create an example of a product experience screen or a help article. That can lead to more aspirational ideas.

Ask for three versions of each example. Encourage writers to scale the intensity of the new voice from low to high. Some sets of examples can be three versions of just a headline, while others may be all the content on a page or screen: title, subhead, bullet text, box labels, button text, etc. Tone can come into play, but voice should be the focus.

This multi-version approach is key to getting to the best content and to getting buy-in from stakeholders.

"I like to mock up copy variations in the prototyping tool Omnigraffle with a screenshot of the actual feature or page," says McAlister. "Then, I create text boxes with new voice and tone variations over the old content so stakeholders can see it in context. I usually do three versions with uniquely angled headlines and value-proposition messaging."

Encourage writers to seek discomfort. If you're doing this as a team, ask each content designer to come back with some out-of-the-ordinary voice examples that may seem impossible, but which will spark discussion about what's on target with your strategy and what's not. Often the crazy, unthinkable ideas lead to innovation.

Workshop your examples

Once everyone has had a chance to mock-up some screens or bits of content and narrow to three versions of each, come back together and workshop the examples as a team. You can display them on a big monitor, but it's much more effective to print them out and put them up on a wall. Put the original next to each set. This is the start of your from-to example set, and it will provide valuable context for what you're trying to do.

Looking at the examples of each piece of the end-to-end experience, ask:

- Which of your principles does it represent? Can you identify an overlap of more than one principle? It's important to clearly see the connection to one or more principles, otherwise it's not strategic, just a new idea.
- Is there something human or emotional in play? Even if you have associated each example with one or more principles, it's a good idea to push for an emotional connection, like excitement, passion, or commiseration. Examples should be inspirational.
- Does it inspire a big change? Will your team see the possibilities?

- Does it align with your overall brand character? Your strategy must stay true to your brand to maintain trust, and this is especially true for examples of a new voice.

Collaborate as a team to re-write and refine the examples. Use stickies for suggested changes or edit the printouts with a pen. Once you have identified changes, work together to tweak the content. Or break out as individuals and then come back as a team for reviews. Iterate until you land on content you all believe in. Shoot for two or three strong examples for each touchpoint. Ideally, there will be a mix of content, including landing pages, notifications or questions in pop-ups (modals), help articles, buttons, and various types of microcopy.

To present your examples, you can create low-fidelity examples, such as wireframes or sketches, but the most effective examples are mock ups of the finished website or product screens. You should have at least some like that.

Think of these examples both as inspiration and as a tool for your writers—internal and external (agency/contract). They should be strong enough to push the team to do something different, to implement your new strategy, and let go of old habits. And they should serve as a reference, just like a style sheet, for what your voice and tone should sound like.

Present your examples for highest impact

Once you have a strong set of examples that represent a selection of touchpoints from across your end-to-end experience, think about how you're going to present them in your strategy document. Creating from-to examples is a powerful way to communicate your new strategy. Take the original screenshots your team used to create the examples and put them together with your mocks-ups on a slide or one after the other on two slides. Create a half dozen of these you can use when presenting your strategy to leaders and stakeholders. I once gave a presentation to 500 people at a company all-hands, and the from-to examples stole the show.

Building Block 4: The Power of Examples

One powerful way to present your examples is to connect them with your principles. You can do this by creating a slide with one or two examples on it next to the principle or principles it represents. Figure 7.1 shows a principle with an example, and Figure 7.2 shows an example from Intuit.

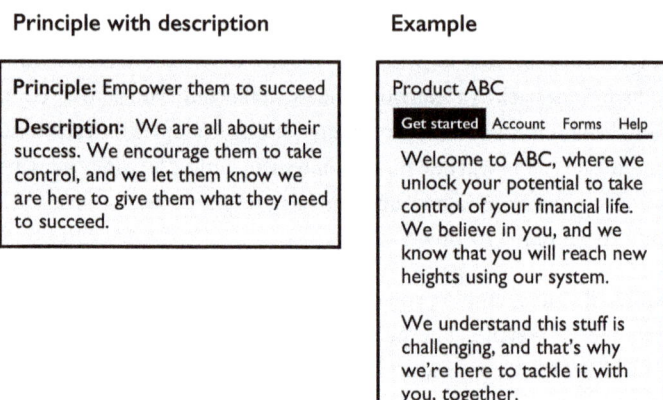

Figure 7.1 – Principle with an example

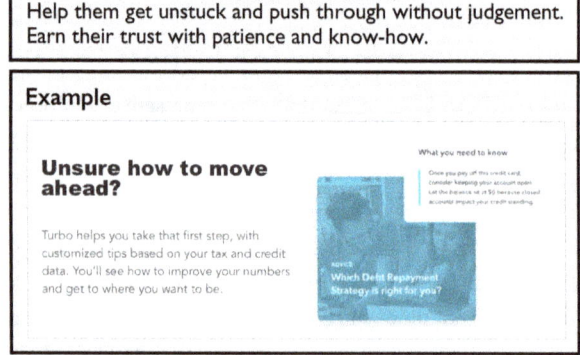

Figure 7.2 – Intuit principle with an example

I've seen this taken to extremes, with examples, principles, and voice attributes all sharing one slide. I recommend keeping it simple. Leave attributes and customer needs for earlier slides. Once you get to examples, the most important connect-the-dots opportunity is a principle next to the actual copy that shows what you mean. If you have separate guidelines for tone, consider using this method for those as well, with an example of a tone flex on a slide with the guideline that describes it.

Another effective tool is the "this, not that" approach I talked about for voice attributes. Figure 7.3 shows the principle followed by "sounds like" and "doesn't sound like" examples.

Principle: Turn self doubt into determination

Sounds like:	Doesn't sound like:
May we use your name and email to send you details about how to use QuickBooks Self-Employed? No spam, we promise.	We need access to your name and email to send you information and instructions for QuickBooks Self-Employed. We will not use this to send you other notifications or messages.

Figure 7.3 – Sounds like/doesn't sound like

McAlister notes that on the fast-paced projects she works on, having a set of "not-this" examples goes a long way toward steering the team down the right path. On a recent email project, she even took some internally generated content that was not on strategy and used it as examples of what not to do.

"I did an audit of some of the emails they were writing," she says. "They were all saying their own things. All my *not* examples were lines taken from those emails. I put those with some 'do this instead' examples and created a set of guidelines. After I gave it to them, I got lots of private messages from the team. They really appreciated it. They took my examples and ran with them."

Use outside examples

Outside examples that show how other companies sound can be useful when making the case for catching up to a competitor or demonstrating how the new voice and tone strategy compares. Consider revealing these at the beginning of your strategy document to set the stage.

Going outside your organization can also help you make examples for specific projects. On her email project, McAlister first looked outside her company for guidance and expertise on what to do. "I Googled a bunch of examples on what makes a great sales email," she says. "What I found helped me write some additional guidelines for the project. I created subject lines, openers, and other content, and shared those with the writers. They were a good addition to our overall strategy document."

Indeed, once you roll out your new voice and tone, you may need to revisit your examples as priorities change and projects come and go. Examples should be the most living part of what will be a living document.

Test your examples

Examples can also serve as a useful tool for testing. Once you get buy-in on the strategic approach, consider working with your research team to do another round of testing with customers. If you don't have any researchers to work with, do some ad-hoc user testing with your new examples.

Take customers to a coffee shop and ask them for their feedback. Observe their behavior and emotions as they read through the content. Ask them why they said what they did or felt a certain way about your voice and tone examples. This can provide great input into the viability and effectiveness of your strategic approach. And, when added to what you learn after rolling out the new strategy, testing can help you make refinements and adjustments to your attributes and principles.

If testing your new voice and tone examples just isn't in cards, don't let it slow you down. "Just be okay with being in the gray," adds McAlister. "I think it's exciting. And it's a metaphor for life. You know what sounds right."

CHAPTER 8
Style and Structure

At the intersection of a voice and tone strategy and a brand strategy is style. Style defines the rules, things like word choice, spelling, grammar, and punctuation. It's how your content and your voice will appear to your customers. Structure defines how you deliver content, including the priority, order, and presentation.

Crafting a voice and tone for your character is about defining the strategy for who you are when you talk to your customers. Style and structure are about delivery tactics—setting the rules and the means by which you will make that voice and tone work.

The guidelines in this chapter do not substitute for any style guide you currently use. They should supplement your style guide and possibly update parts of it. A good style guide that includes recommendations on voice and tone makes the job of the content creator much easier. Creating the aspects of a comprehensive style guide beyond the question of voice and tone is a specialty all its own, which I will not address.[1]

Voice and tone drive style and structure

Style and structure are not purely strategic, which is why they're not one of the strategy building blocks. Voice and tone drive decisions around style and structure, not the other way around.

"All our decisions about content ladder up to voice and tone," says Michael Haggerty-Villa, a style, structure, and systems design expert who has led teams at Hewlett Packard, Disney, and Intuit. "Whether or not you're going to use a serial comma, for example, your voice and tone play into that. The Disney parks don't use it. That's a deliberate choice tied to their voice."

---

[1] Richard Nordquist's article, "What Is a Style Guide and Which One Do You Need?"[25], is a good starting place if you're looking for a style guide.

Haggerty-Villa says he believes Disney decided not to use the serial comma to avoid sounding too formal. At the time, the voice of the character of the Disney theme parks was conversational and magical, and avoiding the serial comma was one—albeit small—tactic they could employ to bring that to life.

Using second person rather than third person is another example of a tactic you can employ to deliver a character's voice. Let's say your attributes and principles are focused on sounding direct and personal. Using second person in your communications is one way to do that. Another organization might pick third person to project a more formal, authoritative voice.

I've worked with several teams that chose to put actions into first person (see Figure 8.1). First person tends to pull the customer into the experience. The result sounds and feels more personal, which can help if you are looking to increase customer engagement.

Do you have a copy of your document?

- Yes, I have a copy
- No, I need to get a copy

Figure 8.1 – First-person query box

Structure can play a similar role. You can choose to structure the question in Figure 8.1 to reveal a follow-up question (see Figure 8.2) only when the customer selects "Yes."

Do you have a copy of your document?

- Yes, I have a copy
- No, I need to get a copy

Is it in electronic form?

- Yes, it's a file or online
- No, it's not electronic

Figure 8.2 – First-person query box with a follow up

Structured content can contribute to a relationship based on personalization. The voice of the character only asks relevant questions. If your principles call for it, you could even give follow up questions in a stronger, more engaging voice with more emotion.

If you don't already have a style guide, make one

Many companies rely on existing and well-established guides for style, including those from The Associated Press (AP), Chicago, or Modern Language Association (MLA), for the majority of everyday writing decisions. But even if one of these guides covers the majority of what you need, you still need to document exceptions that align with your brand identity and your voice and tone strategy. Your strategy will dictate when you stray from what would traditionally be considered correct.

"There are people who are all about the mechanics," says Haggerty-Villa. "They're all about the right way to say something. But even they know that their voice and tone strategy requires them to deviate from being absolutely correct."

One of the first things I coach people is that a style guide is just a guide. It is not black or white. There's room for variation and addition based on what's best for your customer. You can put forth what appears to be a hard rule about abbreviations, but if that rule forces you to ignore what you know about your customer, then it's okay to deviate.

I can recommend two broad approaches for structuring your style guidelines:

- **Industry guide + a list of exceptions and additions:** Use an industry-standard style guide as your main reference and provide a short list of exceptions. Let's say you get most of what you need from the Associated Press (AP) style guide. You could offer that publication and then create a list that highlights the deviations and additions needed to align to your voice and tone strategy.
- **A custom guide:** Create a guide that includes both voice and tone guidance and traditional style recommendations. Such a guide would include guidance on specific words and phrases as well as instruction on topics such as capitalization and punctuation. This will give your teams a single source of truth as they're writing and reviewing.

Once you have your style guide, it's a good idea to introduce it with a section that defines style and structure and describes why they are important. Consider following that with a quick reference guide, which I'll talk about in a bit.

Create a word list

Perhaps the most useful part of any style guide is a word list, a table containing an alphabetized list of words, acronyms and other short phrases you use next to a list of those you don't. This is where things go from suggestions to hard and fast rules. I know I told you that style guides don't contain black-and-white rules. And that's true, except for your word list. This is where you put forth a list of things that are expected to be used exactly as listed.

A good word list uses the same "this, not that" format I suggested for attributes and examples. Using your style list as a guide, create a table that shows correct usage next to incorrect usage (see Figure 8.3 for an example of a word list).

Use this...	Not this...
appear	display
bookmark (one word)	book mark
CPU	central processing unit
choose	select
dealer	reseller
FAQ	frequently asked questions
info	information
and so on...	

Figure 8.3 – Example of a standard word list

Create a quick reference guide

Another useful tool I've offered to my writing, design, and development teams has been a quick reference guide that calls out the most important rules, with an eye on voice and tone. It gives everyone a way to quickly cross-check bits of content as they review designs and recommend content changes, while reducing unnecessary back and forth on word choices and grammar decisions.

A good quick reference sheet often comes in the form of a "language and style top ten," "language quick hits," or something similar. Try and keep it to the length of a standard page. Pull out bigger, more categorical things, like capitalization, pronoun usages, and abbreviations and put them in your top ten. I've often found that the questions raised the most by various team members, peers, and stakeholders can help you decide what to put in your top ten.

A typical rule for your top ten is the use of sentence case versus title case in headings. For a long time, the teams I was working with used title case—capitalizing every word in a title or label—for headings. Around 2010, we decided to switch to sentence case—lowercasing all but the first word. The change led to confusion and conflict. Some people wanted to stick with the old way, while others understood the need to modernize and evolve in line with our new voice. Still others were concerned with the inconsistencies created as we slowly transitioned thousands of marketing and product screens to the new style.

I created an entry in my top 10 style list that read like this:

> Sentence case vs. title case
>
> We use sentence case for all titles, labels, and bulleted lists. This means we capitalize only the first word in a title, label, or list item, and lowercase all other words. Our style is: "Let's fill out this form," not "Let's Fill Out This Form." We realize there are many screens and flows in our product that use the old style of title case and that we can't change them all at once. So, as we review, update, and create new content, follow these rules: Use sentence case for all new or updated content when it's possible to also update the other screens for the most common use case within that flow or task. Stick with title case if switching to sentence case might cause confusion for the customer.

Other helpful items I've pulled out and put in my top 10 lists have included use of the royal we to describe actions ("We'll work on that in a bit"), capitalization rules, and how to spell out numbers.

Set rules for structured content to establish your voice

Just as style can support and build the relationship with your customers, structure offers endless tactical opportunities to connect with your customers. Imagine you're a docent taking people on a tour of a historic house with many rooms containing lots of furniture, paintings, and other objects. You need to structure your presentation so that it makes sense to your visitors. They've come there wanting something from the experience—perhaps some kind of inspiration or maybe just simple amusement. As you guide them through, your voice may be human, clever, or even funny. But you must also structure your presentation to be accessible and understandable.

Structured content is information made useful by organizing and presenting it in a predictable way. Content designers figure out what customers want and what they're trying to do, then structure the words, links, images, buttons, etc., accordingly.[2]

So, what's relevant about structure for those of us crafting voice and tone strategies? Structuring content lets us build and evolve the relationship with our customers. And, more significantly, it's how we address the optional nature of the emotional connections we're trying to create. Not everyone needs or wants you to address their emotional needs. For those who are open to it, you can create lasting connections and meaningful benefit. But for those who desire a purely transactional relationship, you need to provide some opt-outs along the way to streamline the path. That's where structure and architecture come in.

Back in our imaginary historic house, where you're the docent and your customers are tourists, not everyone may want to go down to the kitchen and learn about how meals were cooked in some bygone era. You can force them to go along, but you risk having them tell their family and friends later that the home tour was boring. What if you offered them the option to finish the tour early or continue on to a tour of the kitchen?

Your product or website can do the same thing with the right structure. Chunks of informative content, inspirational messages, or educational flows where voice and tone are designed to connect with emotional needs can be designed using progressive reveals or in second-tier screens behind

---

[2] For more information about structured content, see *Structured Writing: Rhetoric and Process*[5] by Mark Baker. For more about information architecture, see *Information Architecture: For the Web and Beyond*[28] by Rosenfeld, Morville, and Arango.

links. Discovery-based learning is about structure. People can be enticed into learning something new without being taught. Or they can skip past.

If your character's voice is defined as casual and friendly, supported by a set of principles that guide you to sound conversational and speak to emotional needs, asking your customers to slog through a long license agreement in the middle of your relationship with them could be disruptive to your strategy. One structural tactic used by many companies to address this is to make reading the agreement optional. Figure 8.4 may seem simple and common, but it's a powerful example of how structuring content can maintain a relationship built on the strategic use of voice and tone.

Figure 8.4 – License agreement panel

Whatever you're trying to do, content decisions about structure and architecture, just like those for style, are made with voice and tone in mind, Haggerty-Villa reiterates. Everything needs to work together. He says, "But some of those structural decisions are informed by your bigger content strategy. At that broader level, above just thinking about voice, you will consider your problem space, and what your customers are coming to you for. You're not going to have numbers comically bouncing in a website for accountants, nor are you going to structure it like a silly game."

Allow style and structure to evolve

Whatever your approach, treat your style and structure guides as living documents. It's a good idea to regularly re-visit them to make changes and additions. Have discussions around trends in language that affect style—for example gender inclusivity—and incorporate the results into your guide.

Millennials and Gen Z'ers are driving a lot of change in style and structure. "People now have different expectations of content than just 6 years ago," Haggerty-Villa says. "It's changed so much. There are huge changes in the language. How we maintain our voice and tone and credibility in the context of those changing expectations is the challenge. We need to keep up. It becomes an extra burden to be on point with our voice, especially with social media. People share everything now. Customers are breaking our content up into little pieces and sharing it. And we are too. We're creating these tiny pieces of content that will be shared all over the Internet."

One final bit of advice on your in-house style and structure guides: How they're written and presented should represent, as much as possible, the style and voice you are asking your writers and designers to create. The titles and copy in your style guide descriptions should reflect the rules they are talking about. And the entire document should represent the voice and tone you are looking to achieve.

CHAPTER 9
The Roll Out

Rolling out your new voice and tone strategy can seem as big a challenge as creating it. You can't just call a meeting and say, "Look! We've got the answer. This is what you need to do." You'll likely be met with skeptical teams and leaders with conflicting priorities and goals.

The best way to roll out a new strategy will vary depending on the culture and organization of your company. In this chapter, I explore some of the techniques that I have found to be useful.

Create a presentation that tells the story of your strategy

Storytelling is how humans communicate. It's how we make sense out of complicated things, using characters and events to create a narrative that connects with people. The story of how you came up with your strategy is a narrative that includes transformation for your business and revelations about your customers. Put together a slide deck that walks your audience through the story of how you arrived at your strategy for voice and tone. Consider starting your presentation by framing up your new strategy as a journey.

"We're on a journey together, all of us in this room," I like to say, "one that will take us to new heights, but also allow us to learn and grow as a business. This strategy represents the start of that journey, not the end."

You've already got the substance of what needs to go into your strategy presentation: the building blocks of your voice and tone strategy. To turn this into a story, think about the narrative it represents. What was the call to adventure? Why did you and your team accept the call?

Put together some slides that show this call to adventure, the reason for developing your new strategy. Like the diners at the taco truck in Los Angeles, your audience is looking for a connection. Establish it up front, then stitch your building blocks together with some additional bits of storytelling. Here's how it could go:

Introduce the idea of change

Consider starting with a thought-provoking quote from a known source:

> Progress is impossible without change, and those who cannot change their minds cannot change anything
> —George Bernard Shaw

Part one: Lay out the case for change

- Show the ordinary world in which your product lives now. Maybe your website or product was doing OK, but that couldn't last forever. Or maybe your teams have gotten comfortable with what they were doing and need a push to start innovating. This is where you lay out the problem before hitting them with your solution.
- Consider talking about what drove you to do this. Did it include a need to stay ahead of competitors? Was there an inciting event—maybe a new ad campaign from a competitor—that pushed you to go on the journey.
- You want to grab people with emotion, not numbers, so take the time to walk people through the setup, but don't overwhelm them with data.

Part two: Who was involved in the project from the start?

- Put together a slide or slides with profiles of the people who worked on the project. What were their roles and why were they chosen to be on the team?
- Include photos of your team in brainstorm sessions or talking to customers. Pull your audience into the story of what you did.

Part three: How did you come up with your goal?

- What is the goal, and why is it the right goal for your team and your business? How is your company uniquely qualified to achieve this goal?

At Intuit we decided that relationship building through emotional engagement was our best shot at beating our competitors, who were focused more on data and artificial intelligence. That's why content was key for us.

- How is your goal informed by your customer's emotional needs? How is it tied to the common fears and aspirations we all share? The more you can tie your goal to some universal truth, the more your strategy will ring true.
- How does your goal connect to your case for change or your company vision? Part of the narrative is making the connection to the bigger picture of what your company is trying to do.
- What sources of inspiration did you use? Books, videos, TED talks, etc.

Part four: Your customer is the hero of your strategy

- What is the current relationship between your product or service and your customers? Is it purely transactional or does it go beyond that? What needs to change?
- As part of the change in relationship, why does your customer need to be the hero?
- How does your goal connect to your case for change or your company vision? Part of the narrative is making the connection to the bigger picture of what your company is trying to do.
- Lead into your first building block: customer needs and desires, plus the needs and desires of your character. Highlighting your own desires in addition to your customers' desires helps make the new relationship between you and your customer seem human and real. Building a new, more human relationship with your customers with desires met and expressed through voice and tone is the beating heart of a good strategy.
- Hook them with the idea that we're all human, which makes us a bit crazy. But understanding that means we can create voice and tone that can resonate. This is a good place to show the list of customer needs and desires and your character's desires (see Figure 9.1).

Company vision:		
Become the most engaging consumer software solution in the world		
Goal for voice and tone:		
Go beyond the transactional to create a human-like relationship		
Customer needs:	**Customer desires:**	**Your character's desires:**
1. I need you to speak my language
2. I need you to guide me through each task
3. I need you to demystify complex things
4. I need to maintain control
5. I need you to help me get unstuck	1. I want you to treat me like a smart adult
2. I want to feel supported by you
3. I want to define what success feels like for me
4. I want you to turn my fear into ambition
5. I want you to recognize my sense of purpose in life	1. I want to help our customers succeed
2. I want to inspire the customer to feel confident
3. I want to be their go-to source for information
4. I want to create a safe place for the exchange of info
5. I want to turn their negative feelings into positive ones

Figure 9.1 – Customer needs and desires

Once you've established a solid narrative for the story of your strategy development, present your character attributes and the principles you will follow to bring that character to life through voice and tone. But don't linger on them. You are the best judge for how much introductory material your audience will want. As with customers, some audiences will want a narrative and a build-up, and others will want to go straight to the examples.

Even for audiences that want a narrative, it is good to quickly get to the examples that show the solution you're proposing.

At the end of your presentation, illustrate with content and language what the changed world will look as a result of your new strategy. For example, you customers will be:

- Much more loyal, while feeling something positive
- Telling people they love your product
- Tweeting snippets of your voice and tone to their friends
- Sending you messages about how you've changed their lives for the better

I know this can seem a bit dramatic, and there's a risk of your presentation ending with something cheesy, so use your editing skills and your knowledge of your audience to exercise some restraint. However, you need to show something that reveals the transformation your strategy has the power to deliver, even if it's just one slide with a single positive tweet on it.[1]

Take your presentation on a road show

Once you've created your presentation, it's a good idea to take it on a road show to the teams who will be involved in its implementation. Doing a road show can get you buy-in from all the important leaders and teams in a relatively condensed time frame, which should lead to quicker adoption.

Pick one or two people to go on the road show with you. Consider including someone from outside your content team who was instrumental in helping to formulate your strategy, such as a marketing or product manager. This will demonstrate the collaborative nature of what you've done.

Meet with the sponsor(s) first to make sure you have their input and support. Then take what they tell you and incorporate it into your presentation before sharing it with other key stakeholders and teams.

---

[1] There are many good books about building presentations based on storytelling. I recommend *Resonate: present visual stories that transform audiences*[13].

Be proactive and deliberate with your road show. Let people know this strategy comes at the request of your sponsors, and that they expect the organizations you're presenting to to make time for you to present the strategy.

Encourage feedback on your proposed strategy. Engage in some Q&A. Make sure everyone grasps what you're proposing, but also let them know their feedback will be incorporated into the strategy. The more they feel like they own it, the more likely they are to become an advocate. If someone expresses deep interest, consider asking them to join your strategy team and become involved in revisions and updates.

Start working with content creators to get things rolling

Once you feel like you have at least a tentative green light from the stakeholders who saw your road show, start working with the people who need to apply the strategy. Find out what tools they need from you. You've got your presentation, but you still need to create resources that writers can use every day. Some may already be working on the just-dos I discussed in Chapter 7, so they could be well prepared to help you figure out the best tools for them to use.

It's tricky, says Julie Newcome. You don't want to provide too much guidance. In the past, Newcome re-examined her voice and tone principles after sharing the strategy with the writers. "We were going from our broadest picture, which was our character archetype, to our principles. But we needed to make the strategy into something you can hand someone that they can actually work with."

Newcome's team started by giving writers just the principles and asking them to try them out. "To be successful we have to give them a practical way to apply the strategy, not just learn it, or understand it," she says.

She and her team at Ultimate Software carefully selected the projects and customer touchpoints that would initially get the new voice and tone treatment. This allowed them to grow into their strategy at controlled pace and gave them time to learn the best ways to make it happen.

"People will get excited about the strategy, and they will want to use it," Newcome says. "But they may not be ready for it. I like to say, 'hold on, back the truck up.' You need to know when to apply it. The best design is never going to go anywhere if you don't know how to implement it. And you need to test it."

Indeed, your roll out is not only about getting buy-in and creating a useful tool, it's also about starting the process for testing your strategy. You need to ask teams using the strategy to share what they have learned.

Use what you learn and start version two

Start thinking about, and gathering feedback for, the next version of your voice and tone strategy right away. That often starts with the question: How do I know my content is working? Is our content achieving our goal?[2]

Measuring the success of your voice and tone strategy is challenging. Establishing a connection between voice and tone and the success of your product or service can be an exercise in guesswork and assumptions. Look for customer responses in social media, Net Promoter surveys, and observations made in a variety of user research sessions, both scientific and guerilla. What customers say about your voice and tone, how they describe your character's voice in unprompted ways, is the most telling.

What's more, the writers and content designers who are applying your strategy will get feedback from customers directly and through other sources, such as market research. This is valuable input into the next version of your strategy. It may be hard to establish a solid connection between the roll out of your strategy and success metrics such as conversion, but your writers will give you what you need to fine tune or even reimagine your voice and tone to get maximum impact.

---

[2] There are many good articles and blogs on measuring your content, including "How to measure content"[20] by Rachel McConnell and "Measuring your "Return on Content": How to tell whether your content is successful"[19] by Hilary Marsh.

Don't be surprised or discouraged if you need to roll out the next version of your new voice and tone strategy in less than a year. When we created the framework for TurboTax, we needed to do an update to incorporate voice flexes soon after we rolled out the first version of our strategy. Take the lessons you learn and make revisions as needed.

Strategy is king. Spread the word

You've created a new strategy. You are helping your teams be strategic. This is among the most awesome things you can do. Without a strategy, you're just throwing stuff at the wall and hoping it sticks. And that can lead to failure.

Even if you can't get concrete measures of how well your strategy is helping your business, simply being strategic in creating a customer-backed strategy always wins over trying to fly in the dark.

And the more feedback you get on your strategy and your content the better. Feedback can lead to new strategies, so accept it at every turn.

"On one of my projects, there was a period of time where the team was experiencing close scrutiny of the content from senior leadership," says Karin Ikavalko, who has developed voice and tone strategies for major corporations. "This can feel so demoralizing. But the bright side of the criticism is that it showed interest. It showed that the leaders recognized the power and potential of language to shape and impact how customers engage with product experiences. Our content design director helped steer the ship and use this moment to find out more from our senior leaders, and it spawned a major initiative around strategy for voice and tone."

For years, I was a UX writer and content designer, but not a strategist. Based on random observations and data collected through common means, I guessed what customers wanted and wrote words I hoped would give them what they needed to complete a required task. Then I realized that we were missing an opportunity.

Some very smart and perceptive people taught me that content could be powerful, including the kind of content I was creating. No matter how small, or seemingly insignificant, it could connect with people. It could make them feel something positive, become part of their story, and even change their lives. But only if it was strategic. When we understand what people want and then talk to them in a way that connects with their innermost desires, we are doing just that. We are strategists.

CHAPTER 10
Epilogue

As you start the journey of crafting a strategy that can create meaningful connections with your customers through content, I'd like to leave you with a few more tools and trends to consider.

Master the power of story

Everything I've presented in this book is in some way rooted in storytelling. Deep customer empathy, character, voice, and meaningful relationships all come from stories. Throughout history, nothing has created more human connection, brought more people together, and facilitated more change than storytelling. It is the oldest form of communication and still the most effective. Stories make sense out of words.

If your goal is to connect with people in meaningful ways and influence their behavior, you must learn from and leverage stories that resonate. Most good stories aren't just about mystery, adventure, or conquest. At their heart, they're about the relationship between two characters. Treating the relationship between the character in your product's voice and the character of your customer as a story—one that builds and develops—will make a big difference for your business.

To be clear, I'm not talking about turning your product into a screenplay. I'm talking applying storytelling rules and techniques to create connections with your audience through voice. I encourage you to read my post "What storytelling means to voice and tone strategy"[8] to understand why voice and tone works and how it resonates with people.

The future of voice and tone could be AI

Artificial intelligence (AI), usually in the form of chatbots or voice-based user interfaces, can be part of a well-crafted voice and tone strategy. In a world full of devices that can understand human speech, content designers are starting to add *conversational design* to their repertoire.

Relationships between humans and robots (physical or digital) must be built on something that seems authentic. The humorous and endearing humanoid robot character, C-3PO, from the Star Wars movies would mean nothing to the audience if his voice lacked a character with qualities we recognize and find attractive. The humanness of C-3PO's voice—combined with his quick-wit, mannerisms, and the way he leverages voice and tone—makes it work. Even C-3PO's companion robot R2-D2 comes alive with carefully crafted beeps and whistles that make his character seem human.

Text-based *Conversational User Interfaces (CUIs)* include chatbots and support widgets. A good CUI has a unique voice that balances straightforward guidance and personality. Figure 10.1 shows how content strategists can push the limits to great effect.[1]

Figure 10.1 – Poncho

The Poncho character in this once-popular weather app had a human-like personality, including the ability to dodge questions it didn't understand. Poncho's voice and tone were clearly part of a strategy to connect with people through lighthearted and sometimes snarky content.

Voice-based CUIs are best known by products such as Apple Home Pod, Amazon Echo (family of devices), and Google Home. These require strategies that align with existing brands.

"Voice character is still an evolving area," says Lee Engfer, a senior editor at Mayo Clinic, who has been crafting healthcare content for many years. "We're keeping it in line with what we know about our brand. We're walking the line between friendly and informal, but also being authoritative and trusted. And with voice, there's a little more room for fun."

---

[1] Alex Debecker, "How to Craft a Chatbot Personality (without damaging its performance)"[11].

Engfer's team built a first aid tool for Amazon's Alexa and Google Assistant to help people with self-care instructions for common mishaps and other situations. The team learned many lessons and influenced what was a very traditional brand in new directions.

"In our written content, we always used the pronouns he or she," says Engfer. "But for voice we now use they. We just think it's more conversational, and we have the added benefit of it being gender inclusive."

In these examples, the customer asks questions of a robot, and the robot responds. But as with C-3PO, a robot won't connect with people unless it engages in a human-like manner.

Whole books are being written on how to connect with people through a *chatbot*. Erika Hall stresses the heightened importance of human-like language in her book *Conversational Design*[15]. "The way humans use language—easily, joyfully, sometimes painfully—should anchor the foundation of all interactions with digital systems," she says.

Finally, have a look at my strategy for this book

When I set out to write a book about voice and tone strategy, I thought about what strategy I would use to talk to you, the UX writers and content strategists who are looking to get better at the craft of voice and tone. Like any product, website, or campaign, this book project has a goal, which calls for a character and some principles for voice and tone that can create a meaningful connection with the reader.

Table 10.1 shows the strategic framework I put together to guide me in how I talked to you, my customer, throughout this book. It doesn't represent everything I used as a guide. But it did serve as a base for getting started. I encourage you to use this framework as a starting template for your voice and tone strategy, whether it be for marketing pages, a product, an online service, or an enterprise site. Once you have these basic components, you can add elements such as "this, not that" guidelines, additional principles, flex frameworks, and from-to example sets.

Table 10.1 – Strategic framework for this book

Product		
A book on how to craft a strategy for voice and tone		
Goal		
Turn content strategists and writers into masters of voice and tone		
Customer needs	**Customer desires**	**My desires**
■ I need to create customer experiences that are more than just transactional ■ I need to help my design team solve big customer problems ■ I need to engage my customers in a relationship that lasts ■ I need to help my content creators be strategic	■ I want customers to love our product ■ I want content that differentiates us from our competitors ■ I want to elevate our content to a position of influence on the design team ■ I want to be a master of strategic thought	■ I want you to be able to craft game-changing voice and tone ■ I want you to be strategic ■ I want you to understand the purpose of voice and the power of storytelling ■ I want you to become an advocate for voice and tone in website and software design

Character: The design coach

Unlike someone who coaches sports teams, my character coaches designers and writers in design thinking and design craft, including how to develop a voice and tone strategy.

I use my extensive experience, while leveraging the expertise of others, to empower people to succeed. But I'm also in the trenches, discovering, learning, and becoming an even better strategist myself.

Voice attributes

When I speak, I sound…

Knowledgeable	Authoritative	Inspiring
I use my knowledge to give my readers the tools and methods they need to succeed at crafting a successful voice and tone strategy. But I don't overwhelm them with too much information.	My extensive experience qualifies me to advise and instruct writers in this craft, and I am confident in what I tell them. But I never sound arrogant or righteous when talking about what to do.	I believe in my readers and emphasize the opportunities they have to succeed in their craft. I'm always ready with an anecdote or example that can help them see a more awesome future.

Epilogue

Principles for voice		
I bring my character to life when I use my voice to…		
Connect outside experts with my own experience	**Talk about and highlight successes**	**Use examples to show the power of voice and tone**
Knowledge is gained by learning from others. As I teach my readers, I want them to know where I gained my knowledge, how I use it, and why I trust it.	Help people see the power of these tools and methods by sharing my own success and what I have learned. Use similes and analogies when appropriate.	Inspire the readers of this book with evidence that strategic voice and tone works and talk about it in a way that expresses my own passion for it.

Examples		
"Some very smart and perceptive people taught me that content can be powerful, including the content I create. Content can connect with people. It can make them feel something positive, become part of their story, and even change their lives. But only if it is strategic."	"Like a perceptive friend who senses an emotional need, the voice of the TurboTax character met and even exceeded our customer's expectations, eliciting emotional connections between our customer experience and our customers."	"Here's a framework that can help you define high-level flex attributes along with supportive voice attributes that target customer needs and desires at particular touchpoints. It doesn't ignore what you've already defined at this point, but rather incorporates it into the flex framework by designating it as a higher-level set of attributes."

Acknowledgements

I would like to thank the following people for adding their wisdom, advice, and expertise to this book by taking the time to do in-person interviews with me. Unless noted otherwise, all quotes from these experts came from my interviews with them.

Deborah Bosley: Owner of Plain Language Group.

Wendy Castleman: Researcher, professor, and founder of Developpeople UX.

Danielle D'Agostino: Content designer and strategist at Intuit, Instagram, Amazon, and others.

Lee Engfer: Editor and writer at Mayo Clinic and others.

Michael Haggerty-Villa: Content designer and strategist at Disney, Intuit, Hewlett Packard, and others.

Karin Ikavalko: Content strategist at several major corporations.

Michelle McAlister: Content designer and strategist at Intuit, LinkedIn, Airbnb, and others.

Julie Newcome: Content strategist at Ultimate Software and others.

Susan O'Connor: Writer, professor, and storytelling coach.

Carol Valdez: Content designer and strategist at Amazon, Intuit, Petco, and others.

Bobbie Wood: Content designer and strategist at Google, Intuit, and others.

References

We use a link shortener in print because some of the links are extremely long. If you go to https://xmlpress.net/vat/references, you will find a list of references with the complete, un-shortened URL for each.

Cited References

[1] Aaker, David A. *Building Strong Brands*. 2010. Simon & Schuster UK.

[2] Adams, Kristina "What is Voice and Tone? (And Why Should You Care)?" September 18, 2018. The Writer's Cookbook. https://xplnk.com/5vb6j/

[3] Ariely, Dan. *Predictably Irrational, Revised and Expanded Edition: The Hidden Forces That Shape Our Decisions*. 2010. Harper Perennial.

[4] Baeck, Aline and Wendy Castleman. "2x2 Method for Narrowing." 2011. Vimeo. Video. https://xplnk.com/us7o4/

[5] Baker, Mark. *Structured Writing: Rhetoric and Process*. 2018. XML Press.

[6] Berman, Alison E. "The Motivating Power of a Massive Transformative Purpose." November 8, 2016. Singularity Hub. https://xplnk.com/03s2q/

[7] Caldwell, John. "Provocation Can Lead to Emotional Design." August 13, 2015. UX Magazine. https://xplnk.com/mzlfy/

[8] Caldwell, John. "What storytelling means to voice and tone strategy." 2020. https://xplnk.com/aoloy/

[9] Camp, Jim. "Decisions are largely emotional, not logical." June 11, 2012. Big Think. https://xplnk.com/2mh0u/

[10] Campbell, Joseph. *The Hero with a Thousand Faces*. 2008. 3rd edition. New World Library.

[11] Debecker, Alex. "How to Craft a Chatbot Personality (Without Damaging its Performance)." May 15, 2019. https://xplnk.com/7ue2h/

[12] Design Council. "What is the framework for innovation? Design Council's evolved Double Diamond." https://xplnk.com/ybwu5/

References

[13] Duarte, Nancy. *Resonate: present visual stories that transform audiences.* 2010. John Wiley and Sons. https://xplnk.com/s7p5n/

[14] Fenton, Nicole and Kate Kiefer Lee. *Nicely Said: Writing for the Web with Style and Purpose.* 2014. New Riders.

[15] Hall, Erika. *Conversational Design.* 2018. A Book Apart.

[16] Halvorson, Kristina. "What is Content Strategy? Connecting the Dots Between Disciplines." Brain Traffic Blog. October 26, 2017. https://xplnk.com/dsn5m/

[17] Interaction Design Foundation. "What is Emotional Design?" https://xplnk.com/6ezmz/

[18] Intuit. "2x2 Narrowing." December 8, 2014. SlideShare. https://xplnk.com/bn5as/

[19] Marsh, Hilary. "Measuring your "Return on Content": How to tell whether your content is successful." Content Company. https://xplnk.com/qhdiz/

[20] McConnell, Rachel. "How to measure content." Clearleft. https://xplnk.com/nkzt3/

[21] Meehan, Mary. "Don't Mistake Habit For Loyalty: 5 Trends Driving Loyalty Programs That Create Customers For Life." March 27, 2018. Forbes. https://xplnk.com/5j964/

[22] Microsoft. "Microsoft's brand voice: Above all, simple and human." January 18, 2018. https://xplnk.com/1qz6a/

[23] Moran, Kate. "The Four Dimensions of Tone of Voice." July 17, 2016. Nielsen Norman Group. https://xplnk.com/5sw4v/

[24] Moran, Kate. "Tone-of-Voice Words." July 17, 2016. Nielsen Norman Group. https://xplnk.com/6429y/

[25] Nordquist, Richard. "What Is a Style Guide and Which One Do You Need?" March 14, 2019. https://xplnk.com/85e2v/

[26] Owyang, Jeremiah. "The difference between strategy and tactics." January 13, 2013. ThoughtCo. https://xplnk.com/n0vnj/

[27] Perch, Darbinyan. "12 Brand Archetypes Revealed!" The Social Grabber. November 3, 2018. https://xplnk.com/jfyfz/

[28] Rosenfeld, Louis, Peter Morville, and Jorge Arango. *Information Architecture: For the Web and Beyond*. 2015. O'Reilly Media.

[29] Simon, Carmen. "Why People Forget our Content (and what we can do to fix it)." The Content Wrangler. https://xplnk.com/diiq5/

[30] Teodoro, Vince. "Intuit Quickbooks Voice and Tone Principles." Intuit. https://xplnk.com/ljypd/

[31] Walter, Aarron. *Designing for Emotion*. 2011. A Book Apart.

[32] Ward, Melissa. "Don't Stand There With Your Mouth Open." Target Marketing. October 5, 2015. https://xplnk.com/gi1pp/

Glossary

brand strategy

A long-term plan for the development of a successful brand in order to achieve specific business goals. It often includes what a brand stands for and what promises it makes to customers based on their needs and desires. A clearly defined brand strategy provides a foundation for content strategists and designers to connect with customers in a consistent and unique way.

chatbot

A program built with artificial intelligence (AI) to simulate a human conversation. Often used for customer service or marketing systems, a chatbot interface uses pre-determined phrases, auditory responses, or visual cues to answer customer questions, assist in the completion of tasks, or persuade customers to use a product.

cognitive science

The scientific study of the human mind and its processes. By examining the nature, tasks, and functions of human cognition, researchers and designers seek to understand why potential customers behave the way they do so companies can build solutions their customers will use.

confirmation bias

A type of cognitive bias in which people favor information that confirms their existing beliefs or ideas. Identifying this kind of wishful thinking on the part of customers or team members can help researchers and design teams be more innovative, seeking insights and building products that help people move beyond their own biases.

content-first prototype

A prototype that uses content, often in a simple wireframe, to inform design rather than the other way around. Writers create working drafts of content pieces instead of using placeholder words. They then get feedback from customers, which can expose opportunities and challenges early in the content creation process and help interaction and visual designers make decisions about what to create.

conversational design
A craft or discipline derived from UX writing in which human conversation is the basis for language and content crafted for voice-based user interfaces, chatbots, and other forms of artificial intelligence that may not require the use of a traditional keyboard.

conversational user interface (CUI)
A user interface that mimics human conversation in text-based (chatbots) and voice-based (Alexa, etc.) interactions between a computer and a real human. Creating a CUI often requires the creation of snippets of content that are then handled by a natural language processing engine that allows computers to understand, analyze, and create meaning from human language.

customer research
Studies conducted by a researcher or product team to identify customer segments, needs, desires, and behaviors, or to establish the usability of a website, product, or service. Methods include one-on-one customer interviews, observations of people using products (sometimes in a lab), and in-the-wild engagements with people in a natural setting such as a cafe or a shopping center.

marketing strategy
A strategy developed by organizations to give them an edge over competitors, while tapping into market potential. Strategic marketing is used to promote, price, and distribute a product to a specific target market in order to get more sales.

persona
A fictional character created to represent a particular type of customer or user. Personas can assist in identifying ways that someone might use the product or service.

wireframe
A schematic page layout, especially for proposed web content, depicting the interface and navigation. It is normally rendered without color, graphics, or typeface, focusing instead on functionality.

Index

A

Aaker, David, 2
acknowledgements, 105
ad-hoc testing, 78
Adams, Kristina, 4
Amazon Alexa at the Mayo Clinic, 101
Ames, Greg, 26
Arango, Jorge, 85
archetypes, 37–46
    examples, 39
    identifying character using, 38–40
Ariely, Dan, 34
artificial intelligence (AI), 99–101
aspirational principles, 51–54
Associated Press Style Guide, 81
attributes, 37–46
    (*see also* voice attributes)
    character, 37
        presenting, 92–93
    describing, 17
    principles contrasted with, 47
    testing, 45

B

Baker, Mark, 85
Berman, Alison E., 21
Bosley, Deborah, 41, 44
brand strategy, 17, 37, 79
    complementing an existing, 38
    importance of character to, 2
brand, perception of your, 1

building blocks
    customer needs and desires, 13–15, 21–35
    examples, 19–20, 71–78
    principles for voice, 17–19, 47–57
    voice attributes, 16–17, 37–46

C

C-3PO, 100
Campbell, Joseph, 26
Castleman, Wendy, 22, 29–31, 33
Chanel voice, 23
change management, 90–93
character, 1–4
    definition, 3
    voice, 37
character attributes, 37
    flex frameworks and, 59
    presenting, 92–93
chatbots, 99–101
Chicago Manual of Style, 81
content creators
    brainstorming with, 41
    just-dos for, 72
    rolling out to, 94–95
    style guidance for, 79
content strategy, 38
    influence on voice and tone, 86
    voice and tone in a, 4–5, 11
content-first prototypes, 30
conversational user interface, 100–101
customer experience, 6, 13
    end-to-end, 59

Index

customer journey, 6
    end-to-end, 61
customer needs and desires, 13, 21–35
    addressing, 7
    presenting, 91
    storytelling and, 25–26
customer personas, 11, 33
    limitations of, 14
customer research, 11
customers
    as the hero, 91
    connecting through voice, 5

D

Debecker, Alex, 100
Design Council, 10
desires
    as strategic target, 22
    brand, 32–33
    emotional, 27
    examples, 28
discovery-based learning, 86
Double Diamond design process, 10
Duarte, Nancy, 93
D'Agostino, Danielle, 71

E

emotion
    expressed by tone, 4
    using to roll out strategy, 90
emotional design, 13
emotional desires, 27
    examples, 28
end-to-end tone mapping, 65
Engfer, Lee, 100–101
evolving your strategy, 95–96
examples, 71–78
    collaborating on, 75
    creating high-impact, 75
    from-to, 75
    outside, 78
    presenting, 77
    revisiting, 78
    testing, 78
    workshopping, 74

F

flex, 2
    based on product/service, 69
    tone, 65
    voice and tone, 59–70
    voice vs. tone, 68
flex frameworks, 59
    examples, 73
    principles, 64
    voice, 60–63
flex voice principles, 64
framework
    voice and tone, 1, 9–20
        this book's, 101–104
from-to examples, 75

G

goal
    example voice, 22
    presenting your, 90
    voice and tone, 11–13
Google
    I'm Feeling Lucky button, 24
guardrails
    voice attribute, 17, 42–43
guidelines, 79
    tone flex, 67–68

H

Haggerty-Villa, Michael, 79, 86–87
Hall, Erika, 101
Halvorson, Kristina, 4
human nature, understanding, 33
humor
    tone and, 4

I

Ikavalko, Karin, 96
intangible needs, 14, 27

J

just-dos, 72–73

L

Lee, Kate Kiefer, 69

M

mapping tone, 65
marketing organization, 38
marketing strategy, 1
marketing voice, 5–6
Marsh, Hilary, 95
Mayo Clinic, Amazon Alexa at the, 101
McAlister, Michelle, 71, 74, 77–78
McConnell, Rachel, 95
Mint voice and tone strategy, 48
MLA Style Guide, 81
mock ups, 75
Moo.com, 25
mood, 4, 44, 59
Moran, Kate, 66
Morville, Peter, 85

N

narrative, 26, 89–91
needs and desires
    customer, 21–35
    examples, 28
    list of, 15, 27
    narrowing the list of, 31–32
    tangible and intangible, 14
    validating, 29–30
Newcome, Julie, 37, 39–40, 45–46, 94–95
Nordquist, Richard, 79

O

outside examples, 78
Owyang, Jeremiah, 50

P

Perch, Darbinyan, 38
personas (*see* customer personas)
playfulness, tone flex, 68
point of view, 80–81
Poncho (weather chatbot), 100
principles, 47–57
    aspirational, 51
    attributes contrasted with, 47
    crafting for writers, 49–50
    crafting strategic, 50–51
    Microsoft voice, 17
    no-duh vs. aspirational, 53
    subset for projects, 55
    tactical, 55
Proctor & Gamble, 26
product vision, 2, 22
product voice, 5–6
project-specific voice principles, 64
prototypes
    content-first, 30
    example mockups, 74

Q

quick reference, 83–84
Quickbooks voice and tone guidelines, 47

R

R2-D2, 100
relationships, 5
    importance of, 6–7
revisiting examples, 78
road shows, 93–95
role models, 17
Rosenfeld Louis, 85

Index

S

sentence case vs. title case, 84
serial comma, voice and the, 79
Shaw, George Bernard, 90
Shopify
    character attributes, 43
    tone guidelines, 44
Simon, Dr. Carmen, 33
situation, flexing based on, 59
Soup Nazi, 6
speaker
    part of the three S's, 5
Star Wars, 100
storytelling, 89, 99
    discovering desires through, 25–26
strategic framework, 5, 34
    this book's, 101–104
strategy (*see* voice and tone strategy)
structure
    defined, 79
    part of the three S's, 5
structured content, 84–86
style and structure, 79–87
    evolving, 86
style guides, 79
    creating, 81–83
style, defined, 79
substance
    part of the three S's, 5
Sweetgreen, advertisement, 16

T

tactical principles, 55
tangible needs, 27
    examples, 28
    intangible vs., 14
tech-savvy friend, example of archetype, 40
Teodoro, Vince, 47
testing examples, 78
testing, ad-hoc, 78
this, not that method, 20, 77
three S's, 5
title case vs. sentence case, 84
tone, 1, 44
    definition, 3
    flex guidelines, 67–68
    flexing, 60, 65
    mapping end-to-end, 65
tone of voice, 1
top 10 style list, 84
touchpoints, 75
    consistency across, 1
    customer, 6, 56, 94
    flexes for, 61–63
transactional relationships, 85
Trunk Club, 6
TurboTax
    aspirational principles, 53
    list of needs and desires, 15
    principle examples, 19
    voice and tone strategy, 12
    voice flex framework, 62
2x2 narrowing, 31, 41

V

Valdez, Carol, 5
verbs, above- vs. below-the-neck, 54
Vertical Voice and Tone Framework, 10
vision
    connecting goals to, 91
    product, 2, 21–22
voice, 1, 3
    danger of inconsistent, 2
    end-to-end view, 73
    example goal for, 22
    marketing and product, 5–6
    principles (*see* voice principles)
voice and tone
    examples, 73–74
    flexing, 59–70
    strategic foundation for, 34
    strategy (*see* voice and tone strategy)
    style and structure, 79

voice and tone strategy, 47
　attributes in a, 37
　character in a, 38
　customer desires in a, 21
　customer needs in a, 7
　examples in a, 19, 71
　Mint, 48
　outside examples in a, 78
　rolling out, 89–97
　Shopify, 43
　this book's, 101–104
voice attributes, 16
　list of, 40–42
　testing, 45
voice flex map, 65
voice principles, 37, 47–57, 59
　project-specific, 64

Walter, Aarron, 37, 69
wireframes, 30, 75
Wood, Bobbie, 66
word list, 82–83
workshopping examples, 74
writers (*see* content creators)

Colophon

About the Author

John Caldwell is an established content design strategist in the field of software design, including software-as-a-service and marketing. Among his many accomplishments, he has helped teams at top companies craft and govern winning strategies for voice and tone across multiple products and platforms. As the lead for content strategy at Intuit, he created and implemented a bold new strategy for voice that changed the game for TurboTax. John is a writing and innovation coach with more than 20 years of experience. In addition to user experience and content design, he has worked in magazine and broadcast journalism and continues to write on a wide array of topics, from tech to travel.

About The Content Wrangler Content Strategy Book Series

The Content Wrangler Content Strategy Book Series from XML Press provides content professionals with a road map for success. Each volume provides practical advice, best practices, and lessons learned from the most knowledgeable content strategists in the world. Visit the companion website for more information contentstrategybooks.com.

About XML Press

XML Press (xmlpress.net) was founded in 2008 to publish content that helps technical communicators be more effective. Our publications support managers, social media practitioners, technical communicators, and content strategists and the engineers who support their efforts.

Our publications are available through most retailers, and discounted pricing is available for volume purchases for educational or promotional use. For more information, send email to orders@xmlpress.net or call us at (970) 231-3624.

www.ingramcontent.com/pod-product-compliance
Lightning Source LLC
Chambersburg PA
CBHW070556160426
43199CB00014B/2528